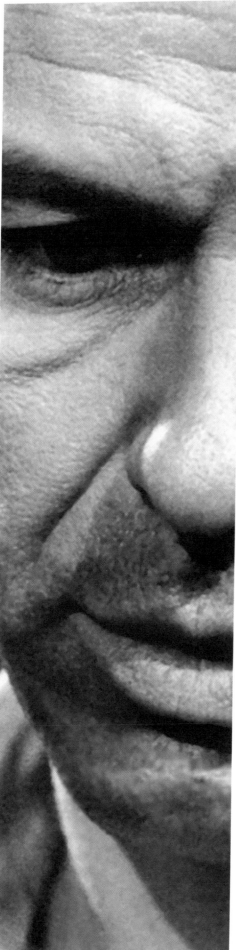

Once in a Blue Moon

The Unforgettable Frank Sinatra

Danann
BOOKS

Danann
BOOKS

First Published Danann Publishing Ltd 2016

CAT NO: DAN0289

Photography courtesy of

Book layout & design Darren Grice at Ctrl-d

Made in EU.

ISBN: 978-0-9931812-7-6

Contents

The Kid from Hoboken

When an Italian immigrant to America, Antonino Martino Sinatra, romantically serenaded Natalina Garaventa and persuaded her to marry him by singing *"You Remind Me of the Girl Who Used to Go to School with Me"*, it might have seemed that their children would be destined not only for delighted parenting but also for musical careers. However, if you were writing a book on how some children have a terrible start in life, you would have to include Francis Albert Sinatra's birth on Sunday the 12th of December 1915 in Hoboken, New Jersey. In fact, Antonino and Natalina's only child almost didn't make it through the first minute. It was a difficult birth because the baby weighed 13.5 pounds, and the doctor had to resort to using forceps to extract the boy from his mother. He had to pull hard on the baby, so hard that the forceps slipped, tearing the child's cheek, neck and ear; when it finally emerged, it was blue and it wasn't breathing. Everyone assumed it was dead.

Quickly cutting the umbilical cord, the doctor put the baby aside and turned his attention to the semi-conscious Natalina. Had it not been for an un-named saviour taking pity on the child and coaxing it into life by splashing water from the sink over it and slapping its back, there would have been no Frank Sinatra.

As it was, both Natalina and Frank survived the life-threatening event, but it was etched into their memories for the rest of their lives.

These were the two most important people in the world that the young Frank had entered; his father, Saverio Antonino Martino Sinatra, who had emigrated from Sicily in 1903 and his mother

Natalina Garaventa, whose parents had emigrated from Liguria in northwestern Italy. Antonino was illiterate, a bantamweight boxer, amongst other things, calling himself Marty O'Brien so that he could enter competitions, because Italians were not wanted in the boxing arenas. But, with the help of his feisty wife, Marty became a captain in the Hoboken Fire Department.

Natalina had been nicknamed Dolly when she was a young child because she was so pretty. As an adult, she was well known in the area because she was not only a forceful and loquacious worker for the Democratic Party, she was a midwife who also offered illegal abortions, a service which landed her with two criminal convictions, but stood her little family in very good stead when the Great Depression hit. This meant that Dolly was always out and about for one reason or another, so between the ages of six and twelve, his grandmother looked after her little boy. When Dolly was at home, however, she was devoted to Frankie. Perhaps over-devoted. Theirs was a fraught relationship. Dolly had wanted a daughter; she bought Frankie pink baby clothes. That wasn't the worst of it, though. When she wasn't mollycoddling him she would hit him; sometimes with a small piece of wood shaped like a bat. Then she would hug him. On one occasion she even sent her son crashing down the stairs.

Presumably he got a hug for that, too.

Little Frankie had inherited his mother's strength of character, but

Above: Italian Immigrants arriving in Ellis Island, New York. The main immigrant entry facility of the United States from 1892 to 1954

Opposite page: Frank Sinatra as a young boy.

while he was an infant, he could not, of course, be the victor in these clashes. But Dolly imbued her son with the same bullying exuberance with which she shoved, carried and led him financially and physically through an extremely difficult childhood.

His mother knew and was proud of her Frankie, though. She said of him later, *"My son is like me, you cross him, he never forgets."* He said of her, *"She scared the shit outta me"*. Little wonder, then, that the adult Frankie was never able to shuffle off the tight coil of this upbringing, and that it set the template for his entire future behaviour.

Dolly's volatile unpredictability left the young Sinatra ever

watchful and unable to be at ease in her company. This unsatisfying first female relationship haunted him always, and blighted his liaisons with women ever after as he desperately attempted to fill the vacuum where trust should have been, often unable to bring himself to rely on it or make himself worthy of it. The uplifting praise and coruscating approbation for failure that was the unwieldy lot of the single child, produced an adult who was unable to be alone, a man teetering over a bottomless pit of need for affection and companionship and riding a big wheel of emotional instability that could soar upwards and downwards almost at the same time.

The ever-resourceful Dolly decided to try and regularise the family's income, and at the end of the 1920s, having borrowed money from her family to do so, she bought a bar in New York and called it Marty O'Brien's. It was to prove the first stepping-stone in the career of the young Sinatra. Initially, though, it meant being looked after by others again; a cousin, his grandmother or Mrs. Golden the Jewish neighbour. But even when the biggest depression in modern times hit America, his mother made sure that her brooding son was well dressed and had enough money in his pocket to attract friends.

The Sinatras lived at 415 Monroe Street in New Jersey. Marty O'Brien's bar at 333 Jefferson St. soon harboured the young Frankie doing his homework and, on occasion, making his way to the top of the player piano to sing for some pocket money from the appreciative clientele. Sinatra was about eleven years old when he realised that he enjoyed singing, was good at it, and that it might be something he could do for money as he got older. It was the last thing his mother wanted for him. She had the immigrant's dream; my son the big shot.

Marty O'Brien's laid the foundation for contact with a less salubrious side of New York life, one that also had a profound influence on Sinatra's life. This was the era of prohibition, after all, and New York's underworld was making millions from selling illegal alcohol. Marty O'Brien's bar, it seems, saw the likes of Bugsy Siegel, the Fischetti brothers, Dutch Schultz and Lucky Luciano people its rooms. Day by day, the young Sinatra absorbed the atmosphere of money, power and self assurance that emanated from these men; is it any wonder that he wished to be like them, that as he grew, his sense of recognition, of belonging amongst them, indeed, of being one of them, might be greater than his sense of belonging anywhere else except on stage.

His mother's odd sense of clothing styles for her son had caused the young Frank to be teased by his peers. She had also spoiled him, and she financed his ever more expensive tastes in clothing. His shyness, quick temper and open emotions did nothing to help him find friends; but his pocket money did. As he grew, he acquired a sense that he was not like the other boys, he was special, and his mother had the same feeling; her Frankie was going places.

Above: Young Frank Sinatra (1st row, R) sitting barefoot in a large group portrait of his family and other guests at the Sinatra family's favorite summer place, the Echo Farm House in the Catskill Mountains, New York. Also shown are his mother Dolly (2nd row, with guitar)

Opposite page: Frank Sinatra poses for a portrait wearing a hat in circa 1922

In September 1927 they all went somewhere; namely, into an apartment on Park Avenue with three bedrooms; it cost $65 a month and Dolly had gained a foot on the first rung of the ladder away from the base of society. For a short while life moved along smoothly; Frankie went to David E. Rue Junior High School, followed by Demarest High School, Hoboken, NJ., Marty went off to be a fireman and Dolly continued hawking her various services around Hoboken. By that time they had acquired another lodger in the house; a cousin of Marty's, Vincent Mazzola, who went under the fascinating nickname of Chit-U. Dolly soon pulled strings to get him a job on the docks, and being the canny wheeler-dealer she was, she took out a life insurance for him, listing herself as the beneficiary.

In this calm before the storm of the Great Depression that began with the stock market crash in America on October the 29th 1929, the young Frankie heard the seductive tones of a certain Bing Crosby on the radio. Crosby's laid-back, intimate style of singing electrified the young Sinatra's imagination. Frank's imagination was already seething with conflicting emotions that ranged up and down the scale between boredom and over enthusiasm, sometimes within a startlingly brief few seconds, and with Crosby's honeyed, mellifluous tones pouring into it, the effect on the teenage Sinatra can only be imagined; it was profound in the extreme.

For the time being there was not much that he could do to move along the route that he now knew he was destined to take, except to keep singing whenever he could. Dolly, ever mindful of his difficulties in acquiring friends, was his cast iron support, as ever, and now she bought him a second-hand Chrysler to try and boost his popularity. Frank was trying his best to court favour with his peers by imitating movie stars and radio comics popular at the time. Still, the word on the street was that Frankie Sinatra was an ineffectual weakling, who tried to bribe the tough guys of the area to be his friends.

In 1931 Frank Sinatra was 16 years old and trouble was brewing. He and his friends would often play truant from school and disrupt the classes when they didn't. He had been at Demarest High School for just forty-seven days when he dropped out, finishing off a less than illustrious educational career with one semester at the Drake Business School. To say that his family was dismayed would be an extreme understatement. There would be no college graduate in the family, no doctor or civil engineer. Dolly was beside herself with rage. Nonetheless, pragmatic as she was, she reconciled herself before too long with Frank's statement that he wanted to be a singer. Marty was adamant though, his son was going to get a real job. If he had prevailed, no one would have known that taciturn Marty O'Brien had single-handedly altered the history of 20th century popular music...

Luckily, Dolly got back on the job.

She stormed the offices of the Jersey Observer and strong-armed the circulation manager, Frank Garrett, little Frank's Godfather, to

agree to employing Frank Jr. to load papers onto a delivery truck; and when a young reporter was killed in a car crash she persuaded her son to go and get the dead man's job. Needless to say, things didn't go well for the unqualified, would-be reporter; when told he had to go, the rejection sent him into a screaming and swearing fit. Not the best of reactions. One that would raise its ugly head on many occasions in the future, however, whenever he was confronted with rejection, authority, was cornered or caught out.

Just how powerful a force Dolly Sinatra was can be judged by the fact that in the face of the biting hurricane that was the Great Depression, she managed to uproot her young family once again, in December 1931, and move to the more up-market area close to the Hudson River, to 841 Garden Street and a house boasting central heating and a telephone. There was no renting this time; she bought the house with a mortgage, which she repaid partly by taking in lodgers. To get her wayward son to contribute to his own or the family's life in any shape or form, she had to work extra hard at finding jobs, in the severe atmosphere of the depression years. But by heaven she did it, and with the help of one of Frank's uncles, Frank found himself working at the Tiitjen and Lang Shipyard in Hoboken in a precarious job, catching white-hot rivets, one of which almost took him down to the bottom of a four-storey shaft. That job went the way of the dodo after three days. He went to work for Lyons and Carnahan, unloading crates of books. That bored him so much he ended up back on the docks with United Fruit Lines unscrewing tubes in condenser units. In the winter it was bitterly cold, icy and it snowed; he wasn't going to put up with that and he was soon idling away his time at home again. This kind of behaviour was too much for his father to bear. Marty abandoned his normally taciturn character and told his son to get out. Under the distraught eyes of his mother, Frank packed a case and left...

He couldn't even make that work, and on Christmas Eve he was back home again. Sinatra, of course, never spoke about what truly happened in that hiatus in which he failed to live up to his own view of himself and his expectations. In later years, the episode would be invested with romance, and became the heart-warming tale of a guy beating the odds with cool nonchalance.

So the year of 1932 slowly unrolled in an unstable young life. If nothing else, the reluctance to work and his inability to stand on his own two feet persuaded his parents, once they had got over their guilt at what had happened, that he really did want to be a singer. They decided that they had better try to support him. The problem was that at that point in time he didn't really have much of a voice. But then, as later, he worked at developing his talents in the hope that he could one day equal his heroes Bing Crosby and Russ Columbo.

With $65 from his parents, he bought a microphone and amplifier, which put him one step ahead of his rivals for singing jobs in the area. The money also enabled him to buy sheet music. All of this, combined with his Chrysler, meant that he started to become a sought-after entertainer, singing the songs made famous by Bing Crosby, in social halls, at school dances and Democratic Party meetings. He was 19 years old; it was time to dream.

In the summer of 1934, Frank took off for Long Branch on the Jersey Shore. And he fell in love.

The story passed down is that Frank, having seen a sweet little seventeen-year-old girl, decided to serenade his way into her heart. So, strumming an accompaniment on a... well, a ukelele, apparently, he crooned that *"It was a lucky April shower, it was a most convenient door"*. The melodious ploy worked. It never failed to work throughout his subsequent career, either. So, the rather inadequate young man now had a girlfriend, Nancy. And with her came her bubbling Barbato family, which he loved to be part of. Soon, he also had another job, because father Barbato had made it absolutely clear that without a proper job he would not be seeing Nancy again.

Frank did well this time. He lasted two weeks.

His first record.

His last 'proper' job.

Father Barbato was not impressed. Nancy's house was now a castle to which Frank was granted no key.

But in the cause of furthering his music career he was no slouch, and he made himself known to anyone who could be of use to him in Hoboken and even managed to squeeze fifteen minutes airtime from WAAT radio station in Jersey City. It didn't lead to fame and fortune. No matter, Frank had a secret weapon.

Dolly.

Thanks to her machinations, Frank was soon giving his all at the Union Club on Hudson Street five nights a week. But then his mother really struck gold and created that all-important opportunity for the first bite at the apple for her wayward son. The Flashes were a trio that played the area with some success, and Frankie wanted in. The boys were reluctant... until Dolly verbally besieged their parents and anyone who had anything to do with them with such force that they all caved in.

Frankie was about to become a pro.

The Flashes came to the attention of Major Edward Bowes, whose NBC radio show, a contest format known as "Original Amateur Hour", was one of the shows that all of America listened to eagerly. Before Frankie knew it, he was the front man for the group, now rechristened the "Hoboken Four", that the Major announced at the Capitol Theatre in New York on the 8th of September 1935. Their song was a cover, "Shine". The audience was delighted with them. So delighted, in fact, that the Hoboken Four won the contest; 40,000 people phoned in. That delighted Major Bowes, too, and he booked the Hoboken Four on a tour. The boys then set off on a coach and train journey, zigzagging across Canada and the States, staying in cheap rooms, hotels and

Opposite page: Frank Sinatra (far right) performing before a microphone with the Hoboken Four, NBC Studios

corner; he headed home.

For the next three years he would live at his parents' house, trying to get his stalled career off the ground.

Sinatra seemed to have taken confidence from the lessons he had learned and the experience he had gained from his months on tour, and with new vigour, he threw himself into the task of finding paid gigs. Even underpaid gigs were acceptable, anything, as long as he could get in front of a microphone and hone his voice into a saleable commodity.

He pounded the streets of Tin Pan Alley and visited the nightclubs on 52nd Street to see what he could learn from the vocal techniques of his rivals, one of whom he revered; Billie Holiday. Not really a rival.

It was during this time that Sinatra met a piano player by the name of Edward Chester Babcock. He would soon be known to the world as

YMCAs. It was a journey that would change Sinatra.

He realised, for a start, that though unformed, his vocal style, paired with his vibrant blue eyes, had a startling effect on women, and he used his newfound knowledge to assist in helping him to investigate the female form after his performances on stage had finished. There was also something else he knew: even though he was only 5 feet 7½ inches tall, he was head and shoulders above his fellow band members in talent. They were aware of the same thing, and driven by jealousy, subjected their lead singer to an occasional dusting down, one of which even led to him being knocked out. So, three months after he had gone out on tour, shortly after his 25th birthday, he sang his last song for Major Bowes and left the tour and the Hoboken Four to fend for themselves. Christmas was around the

Jimmy Van Heusen and become a renowned composer. Van Heusen suggested that Sinatra take singing lessons as his voice still lacked substance, depth and freedom and so for $1 a session, John Quinlan, a New York vocal coach, set to work to produce a voice that would set Sinatra on the road to fame and fortune.

Well, on the road to a job at The Rustic Cabin for $15 a week as a singing waiter and emcee in 1938, at any rate. And even then he had to employ his secret weapon to get it after his audition piece had failed to do its job. But Dolly pulled a few strings in the Democratic Party, the bells jangled in the offices of the musician's union of New Jersey and hey presto...! *"Ladies and gentlemen your favourite band, Bill Henry and his Headliners with Mr. Frank Sinatra"*.

It was learning, wasn't it; it was experience, wasn't it? It was a foot in the door. Wasn't it? If you could never be sure of the world; you had to be sure of yourself.

Frankie had listened and learned from the best in his profession; from the likes of Billie Holiday and Bing Crosby. He had learned to invest the lyrics with meaning and emotion. The result was that he was now the recipient of letters of admiration and love, even house visits, from his female audience at the Cabin. He felt success tingling his fingertips.

His personal life wasn't moving along quite so smoothly. In fact, his train got derailed briefly. Whilst dating Nancy, he had also succumbed to the attentions of a certain Antoinette Della Penta who, as far as Dolly was concerned, was from the wrong side of the tracks and therefore a persona non grata. What was worse was that with Antoinette, Frank had succumbed to his need for sex.

When Nancy and Antoinette crossed paths at the Cabin one night they went for each other, no holds barred. The following night the police arrived in the middle of Frankie's set and arrested him on the spot. At two in the morning he found himself in jail at Hackensack County prison. It was a kick in the pants for the overconfident youngster, who now had to phone his mother to pluck him from the deceitful jaws of his own arrogance once more.

"On November the 2nd and 9th 1938, Frank Sinatra being then and there a single man over the age of 18 years, under the promise of marriage did then and there have sexual intercourse with the said complainant who was then and there a single female of good repute for chastity whereby she became pregnant."

That complaint sent him to prison for 16 hours after his arrest. $1,500 got him out on bail. He was not, however, out of hot water

Opposite page: Frank Sinatra poses for a mug shot after being arrested and charged with 'carrying on with a married woman' in 1938 in Bergen County, New Jersey

Top Right: Billie Holiday at the Club Bali, Washington

Top Right: Bing Crosby

even though it subsequently transpired that Antoinette was already married to a Mr. Edward Franke. The charges were dropped. Unfortunately, the problem refused to lie down. Following another confrontation, this time between Dolly and Antoinette, which ended with Dolly hurling Antoinette into the basement of the house, Antoinette had a second warrant issued against Frank. With the chutzpa and cheek of a woman scorned, she stated the reason this time to be adultery. Once more, Frank was faced with the men in blue just as he was warbling to his admirers at the Cabin. It was Christmas. Once more, Frank had to push the red button to launch his secret weapon. $500 released him from his second incarceration. The case went to trial on the 24th of January 1939 and was dismissed. But Dolly exacted a price for her life-saving interventions; just a few weeks later, on February the 4th, 1939, Frank and Nancy were married at Our Lady of Sorrows Church in Jersey City. The bride was in love; the groom probably loved her love, and certainly his potential career, far more.

Shortly afterwards, Dolly, too, found herself under the gentle protection of the police, who arrested her for carrying out an abortion.

She had no secret weapon to help her out.

Frank and Nancy rented a three room apartmentin Gardield Avenue, Jersey City. Frank continued working at the Rustic Cabin, his fee was raised to $25 a week and he joined guitarist Tony Mottola on a daily radio show, Blue Moon, besides singing at a nightly gig for the WNEW Dance Parade in Manhattan. Nancy worked at American Type Founders in Elizabeth, New Jersey, as a $25-a-week secretary. It could have been a comfortable existence were it not for her husband's insatiable desire for expensive suits, ties, shoes and shirts. Nancy stretched the dollars, putting her own desires on the back burner. A woman in love. There were mighty rows and happy reconciliations. He was a fleeting figure in the house, always needing to be somewhere, meet someone, while she cooked to contain him. An impossibility, of course, to contain the mercurial singer, who already felt trapped, even though he loved the bubble of stability she provided, loved Nancy's generous understanding and warm spirit that buoyed him up in the unforgiving world of snakes and ladders that he was part of.

Would he ever find another ladder? Despite Frank's rock-steady confidence in his own abilities, radio stations and just about everybody else were not so sure. And even he must have wondered, temporarily, what was going to become of him after he managed to freeze up in front of the microphone one night when the famous bandleader Tommy Dorsey dropped into the venue. It was as though fate wanted him to suffer before handing him the riches that would later be his.

Above: Harry James taken from the Billboard 1944 Music Yearbook

Opposite page: Frank Sinatra in a nightclub next to his first wife, Nancy Barbato.

To his credit, Frank didn't give in. And he persuaded the "King of Swing", the immensely talented trumpeter Harry James, to come to the Cabin and listen to him sing. It seems that James's wife, Louise Tobin, had heard Sinatra on the radio and made a remark about him to her husband. James came to watch, and that encounter at the Rustic Cabin led to him hiring a male singer to work alongside Connie Haines for his newly formed band. He paid Frank Sinatra $75 a week, three times his current wage total. It almost went west when James suggested Frank Sinatra became Frank Satin. Job or no job, Sinatra always had a principle that he would not throw to the wolves. He would make the big time on his own terms, no compromise. The name was a deal breaker.

Sinatra turned on his heel and walked off.

James followed him.

On June the 30th 1939, the *"very pleasing vocals of Frank Sinatra, whose easy phrasing is especially commendable"*, stepped out in front of Harry James and The Music Makers at the hippodrome in Baltimore. The girls fell under the spell of the voice at the very first gig and could not restrain the screams.

The long-awaited breakthrough had finally come.

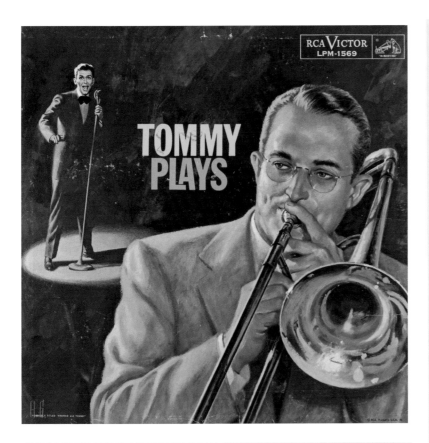

When October 1939 came around, Nancy announced that she was pregnant.

Life on the road with a band that was going nowhere, without money and accompanied by a now pregnant wife, was beginning to make Sinatra very uneasy indeed. It was obvious that if he was going to progress, and there was no doubt in his mind that with the talent he knew he had, he was going to progress, then he and James needed to part company. First of all, he had to part company with Nancy, selling the Chrysler to raise the money for a ticket to send her back home, whilst he and the band staggered forwards on one-off gigs, playing cards, riding the buses and trains.

Sinatra was unaware, but he was about to reach one of those lucky milestones in life that can open doors. Another singer was inadvertently working on his behalf to get him out of the rut he was in; the man's name was Jack Leonard and he sang for an orchestra that Sinatra would likely have sold Dolly into slavery to work for. It belonged to one of the greats of the era.

Tommy Dorsey.

And Jack Leonard had recently left the Tommy Dorsey Orchestra. Dorsey had a temporary replacement but he badly wanted a better singer. Leonard gave the bandleader a soaring recommendation of Sinatra's talent, and when Dorsey happened to hear Sinatra on the radio for himself, singing "All or Nothing at All", it led to Sinatra auditioning for the bandleader in the Palmer House ballroom of the hotel where Dorsey was staying. There was no freeze up this time around. Sinatra made "Marie" pour into the microphone with a rhythmic swing and sweet subtlety to get her to seduce Dorsey's eagle eyes and ears. She did her job to perfection. Dorsey was won over and invited Sinatra to sing with the band. Sinatra was bowled over, as well he might have been. At 24 years of age, Frank Sinatra was finally on his way towards the big time.

Harry James was magnanimous in defeat. He knew what the deal meant to Sinatra and he sent him on his way with a handshake, and with the words *"I think that's what you want"*, he tore up Sinatra's contract with the Harry James Orchestra.

It affected Sinatra deeply when the bus pulled away with the rest of the musicians, at the end of his last gig. He had learned so much from the bandleader, so much about rhythm and phrasing and, indeed, about life. *"There was"*, he said, *"such spirit and enthusiasm in that band, I hated leaving it."* He felt the tears come and was grateful to be going home to Nancy.

But this was a time for looking forward to an exciting, inviting future, and just a few days later Sinatra was on the road again. Except that his new job was light years away from the old one.

But not financially. Harry James found it difficult to keep his band on the road in an era when Count Basie, Duke Ellington, Tommy Dorsey and Glenn Miller filled the airwaves. Nonetheless, Sinatra remembers this period of his life with great affection and as he said, despite the trouble and hardships *"I can truthfully say it was full of happiness"*.

Sinatra went into the Brunswick Studios at 550 5th Avenue on the 13th of July 1939 to cut his first record with the Harry James Orchestra; "From the Bottom of My Heart" with "Melancholy Mood" on the B-side. Despite Sinatra showing that at 23 years of age he was beginning to master his unique vocal ability, neither song went anywhere and the record sold just 8,000 copies. In all, Sinatra released ten tracks with Harry James in 1939, including "All or Nothing At All", which also went nowhere on its release, primarily because the ASCAP (The American Society of Composers, Authors and Publishers) would not allow the recording to be aired on the radio. Four years later when they changed their tune, it became Sinatra's first major success, selling over one million copies.

Opposite page: A young Frank Sinatra in his dressing gown tucks into some bacon and eggs for promotional photo

Top: Album cover of Tommy Plays

Next page: Performing with the Tommy Dorsey Orchestra in a still from the film, 'Ship Ahoy,' 1942

There's only one singer... and his name is Crosby

great man wore. And he, Sinatra, was going to outshine even the great Dorsey; of that he was certain and he continued to hone his own phrasing of a song, the way of telling a story without artifice that went straight to the heart.

By the time the Dorsey band headed towards New York, the singer at the front was not the same boy that had been hired by Dorsey just a short time before. The almost hysterical audience reactions had confirmed to Frank what he already knew; he had that indefinable something that set him apart, he had the soft dawn glow of stardom twinkling in his eyes. Dorsey knew it, too, even if he would never have expressed his feelings, but the fact that he gave Sinatra featured billing in one of the biggest clubs on the east coast spoke far louder than words.

Now, even Sinatra's initial approach to his songs changed.

The era of the phonograph and the radio was well and truly under way and the listening public was hungry for new voices that would bewitch them as Bing Crosby's did. Swing music had gripped everybody's dancing with a vengeance; it was the teenagers' rebellious focal point, and into this vibrant scene dropped the young Frank Sinatra. The vulnerable loneliness and the yearning for love in the startling blue eyes could be clearly seen by every young woman within half a mile of him. The slight quiver in the sensuous lower lip, the slim body, the diffidence, the searching hands and the gentle vocal tones, paired with a unique, silky phrasing, made this singer special and irresistible. But he was also a loner, by his own confession, and the much more rigid discipline enforced by Dorsey made Sinatra homesick for the James band for many months into his new tour of duty as the Greyhound bus ploughed relentlessly through the American night to the next venue.

All the while, though, Sinatra was developing his style, refusing to be bowed by the authoritative figure of Dorsey with whom there were, inevitably, arguments and shouting matches. Yet they both found a way through to each other through their loneliness, playing cards together through the night until dawn broke.

And all the while, Sinatra was listening, watching and learning; learning how Dorsey controlled his singing with his remarkable breathing techniques, how he controlled his band, how he controlled his environment, professionally and personally. Dorsey the man and bandleader impressed the young Sinatra enormously. So much so, that he tried to copy him, even down to wearing the cologne the

His creative brain had understood something vital to his profession. He insisted on being given the lyrics unencumbered by the musical score before he began to study the melody. He would start by simply speaking the words as though they formed a poem. By doing so, he could find his way through to the heart of each word and sentence, each sentiment; unearth the narrative line unencumbered by the seductive curling of the musical accompaniment. For the rest of his career, this was how he would always find his way into a new song. And when he heard the apparently seamless bowing of the inimitable Jascha Heifetz, he wanted to achieve that seamless quality with his voice, and worked tirelessly to acquire the technique of becoming a 'vocal violin'.

By March, Sinatra knew he was on his way; he was a headline name at the Paramount Theater in New York, the greatest big band venue of them all. And the queues around the block, the adoration of his female fans, who couldn't get enough of their idol, told him all he needed to know. His days with the Dorsey Orchestra were already in the autumn of their life.

Frank went into the studio again to start recording the first of eighty-three songs that he would record with the Dorsey Orchestra. Forty of those were cut before the end of the year. The first was "The Sky Fell Down" and "Too Romantic" recorded at RCA in Chicago. In May he recorded "I'll Never Smile Again". It became a smash hit, and as chance would have it, Billboard Magazine had just begun its charting of America's best-selling records. Sinatra came in at number 1 for the inaugural week of July the 27th and stayed there for the following 12. The "bobby soxer" generation had found their darling.

Besides these professional forward strides, Frank was also making personal contacts that would feed into his stage life with men such as Sammy Cahn, and renewing the acquaintance with Jimmy Van Heusen, now also very much on the ascendant as a songwriter.

In May, something extraordinary took place that marked the beginning of the end of the Dorsey/Sinatra swinging steamroller. It was a night never to be forgotten, especially by the singer himself. It was a night of magic when, at the Astor Hotel, Sinatra completely captivated his audience of glittering, wealthy patrons. They wildly demanded an encore; Dorsey allowed them four more numbers, wily showman that he was.

Opposite page: Vintage Radio Advertising for RCA Victor, Circa 1941

Right: Frank Sinatra poses for his first publicity portrait during his stint singing for the Tommy Dorsey Orchestra in New York City

Frank asked for **Smoke Gets in Your Eyes**. None of the musicians could play it. Turning to the microphone, the singer took a breath... and filled the room with the incomparable sound of Frank Sinatra.

Solo.

On that night, a star was born in New York.

No longer was it Dorsey/Sinatra. Even Dorsey had knelt down after an epiphany moment. The skinny kid with the greasy hair was now in out in front on his own in every sense. Nonetheless, he was still only earning a $25 bonus for a recording session, no royalties, and still a long way behind his idol Bing Crosby. Sinatra's ego had gone on ahead as the advance guard to his fame, and he even took to conducting the orchestra if Tommy Dorsey was late, for which crime, Sinatra was not shy to make his feelings known to the great man.

Another momentous moment for Sinatra came just over two weeks later on the 8th of June 1940 when his daughter Nancy was born at the Margaret Hague Hospital in Jersey City, an event that apparently kept him chattering all night about the sweet little addition to his family. Yet Sammy Cahn recalls Sinatra saying that he was unhappy as a married man. Fame was bringing him more pretty girls than even he could deal with in one night. Marriage felt like a stone at the bottom of the swag bag. Only his career mattered, said one of his contemporaries. He had shaken hands with Bing Crosby whilst the Dorsey Orchestra was involved in a film in Hollywood; yes, the Bing Crosby, who had uttered the gold-plated words to him; *"You're going to go far"*. Who could stop him now?

By May of 1941, Frank Sinatra's name and picture were blossoming all over the United States. He was the new singing sensation and was named Male Vocalist of the Year by Billboard in May 1941, squeezing out Bing Crosby. That same month, Sinatra wrote his first song, co-authored with Hank Sanicola, music by Sol Parker; **This Love of Mine** was recorded with the Dorsey Orchestra. The **bobby soxers** were swooning and fainting at his concerts. Sinatra's difficult personality began to get out of hand. The rising star became conceited and abrupt to those around him.

Frank liked to live life in the fast lane, and as far as he was concerned, his personal vehicle had become lodged in second gear. Now, however, his life was about to speed up dramatically.

The band was back in Los Angeles by November of 1941 and Sinatra appeared in what would prove to be his final film with Tommy Dorsey, "Ship Ahoy", starring Eleanor Powell. Sinatra's songs were filmed

with close-ups; the big-time was almost tangible.

It was whilst he was in Hollywood contemplating a bright future that he bumped into a pianist friend from his days with Major Bowes, Lyle Henderson. There was a woman beside him. But this was no ordinary woman.

This was Ava Lavinia Gardner.

Frank was mesmerised and couldn't take his eyes from her. She was 19 years old and had been in Tinseltown for barely four months. On that occasion, she remained in his vision just long enough for him

Right: Ava Gardner

Opposite page: Frank Sinatra - 1942

There's only one singer... and his name is Crosby

Above: Posing for a portrait, 1942

Middle: Recording session for Bluebird Records, a division of RCA

Far Right: 1942 in Los Angeles, California

There's only one singer... and his name is Crosby

to fall into confusion, and then she and Lyle were gone.

There was another meeting that month with someone who would penetrate deeply into Sinatra's life; Emanuel Sacks, known as Manie. Manie was working at Columbia Records as their 'popular repertoire manager', a job title that had Sinatra's ears waggling. Immediately, he asked Manie if he would like to make a solo record with him. Manie had already recognised Sinatra's talent at the Rustic Cabin and didn't hesitate to agree. A bold move by both of them; firstly, because Sinatra wasn't free of Dorsey, and secondly, because singers and bands belonged together. But a solo singer? As though to cast aside any doubts, "Down Beat" named Frank Sinatra as their Male Vocalist of the Year. Surely the die was now irrevocably cast. What could get in his way?

Nothing.

Except, perhaps, a war.

On December the 7th 1941 the Japanese attacked Pearl Harbor and America entered World War II. Sinatra's punctured eardrum kept the Japanese and/or German guns at bay. But who knew what might happen in this world set on fire, and Sinatra brought more urgency to his pleas to Dorsey to be allowed to record as a solo artist. And in 1942, as James had done before him, Dorsey relented and gave his upstart protégé his head.

On January 19th 1942, Frank was ready to record. He was a nervous wreck as he walked into the studio, oozing confidence on the surface, jelly on the inside.

He had chosen romantic ballads; "The Lamplighter's Serenade", "The Night We Called It a Day", "The Song is You", and the song that even the musicians applauded; "Night and Day". That one just had to be a hit.

Apart from the solo recording, the inevitable impending split with Tommy Dorsey was also occupying Sinatra's mind, but negatively. Back in New York, he recorded ten singles with the band; these turned out to be the last that Dorsey and Sinatra would make together. Sinatra was a man in a hurry and in February 1942 he gave notice to Tommy Dorsey, continuing to sing with the band until there were just three months left of his three-year contract to go. Dorsey was doubtless extremely hurt, but he was also worried that Sinatra was making a mistake. If only he could have known. Sammy Cahn thought he knew. So did Lana Turner, perhaps, with whom Sinatra had started an affair, which they continued after his next marriage, apparently, according to Lana's daughter. His marriage to Nancy held no interest for him now, and his two-year-old daughter became used to the war years without him.

Between then and August 1942, Sinatra and the band worked ceaselessly between radio shows and live performances. Yet the bandleader could not disguise his anger at Sinatra's decision to leave, and finally stopped talking to him altogether. To no avail. Finally the two sides came to an accommodation and Sinatra was released from his contract. But not before Dorsey and his manager had squeezed from him a 10% agent's fee to be paid to Dorsey's manager and 33.3% of Sinatra's gross earnings for ten years for Dorsey himself. At least, that's what the words stated.

Sinatra had wangled $17,000 as an advance from Dorsey. He, on the other hand, had not the slightest intention of giving a dime to

...we here highly resolve that these dead shall not have died in vain...

REMEMBER DEC. 7th!

Above: "Remember December 7th" US Government propaganda poster of 1942

Opposite page: Frank Sinatra crouches to kiss his daughter, Nancy Jr., good-bye at a train platform with Nancy

anyone. (A host of stories, all of them involving the Mafia and threats to Dorsey and his family, not to mention his career, went the rounds, speculating on exactly how Sinatra had managed to extricate himself from this noose. Not surprisingly, Sinatra would not say, and the real run of events have gone with him to the grave.) Suffice to say, September rolled around, and after a final radio broadcast on the 3rd, Sinatra finally left the band on the 8th. He was replaced by Dick Haymes, who had replaced him when he left Harry James, too. Dorsey was reported to have said, *"I hope you fall on your ass"*.

For a while, it seemed as though Sinatra had broken free too soon, for while the "bobby soxers" swooned, the rest of America didn't much care about Frank Sinatra. That was until Bob Weitman, manager of the Paramount, was persuaded to use his talents in December 1942. Sinatra landed two gigs at the same time; New Year's Eve at the Paramount backed by Benny Goodman's orchestra, and "Star Spangled Rhythm", a film starring Bing Crosby, Bob Hope and a handful of other Hollywood stars.

Sinatra's fans raised the roof at that Paramount show, the girls thronging in the aisles, screaming through show after show. It was extraordinary. Top showbiz press agent George Evans thought so, too, as he sat through four shows in the sexually-electrified theatre and knew that he was in on the start of something big. Frank Sinatra's voice made love to every woman in the theatre. It wasn't the skinny young man's physique that had them drooling, it was his way with words, the timbre of his voice. The Voice. Evans had hit on the epithet that would be Frank's forever. Thereafter, Evans coached girls in the dark arts of well-timed audience participation; there were many, of course, who needed no coaching. They could not stop themselves from fainting anyway. The two-week engagement was extended to eight and Sinatra's salary soared from $750 a week to $25,000. The phenomenon that was Sinatramania had struck America.

Right: An advertisement awning outside a theater, for the 'Star Spangled Rhythm' concert featuring Benny Goodman and Frank Sinatra, 1940

Fly Me to the Moon

George Evans shamelessly painted an untrue picture of a home-loving young singer caring for his wife and young child, who had risen from a poor but decent background to better himself through education. It was Evans, too, who persuaded Sinatra's wife, Nancy, to pay attention to her looks as a counter-attack against all those pretty young things yearning to get into Frank's bed and destroy the careful picture that Evans was anxious to build up around the singer, to cradle prudish 40s America. He did a good job, because by May 1943 there was another baby on the way for the couple.

Sinatra's star was shooting upwards. "There Are Such Things", a number from one of the last Dorsey-Sinatra recordings, was released in January and fired up to number 1 on the Billboard chart by the middle of the month, taking down "White Christmas" by Bing Crosby.

Manie Sacks had agreed to sign Sinatra, working as his music publisher after the Dorsey contract was over, and now he was one of a group known as the Varsity, Sinatra's very own entourage that also included Sammy Cahn and Jimmy Van Heusen. Even at that early stage they called him *"the Monster"*; driven, tied to the whims of an unbridled temper, exhibiting unconcealed impatience, displaying unbounded arrogance. A bully; son of Dolly.

The boy who wanted it all had his first million seller with a song he had recorded with Harry James in 1939, "All or Nothing at All". It was released in March 1943. More sold-out shows followed in May at the Paramount.

By August, riding on the wave that baffled everyone except

Sinatra, Frank was back on the West Coast to sign a seven-year movie contract, and singing at the Hollywood bowl to 10,000 enthusiastic spectators. In October, "Songs by Sinatra", a 15-minute weekly radio spot on CBS began, with Sinatra as the star. This was soon followed by "Higher and Higher", Sinatra's first film under a new RKO contract and an eye-opener for everyone; he had presence, he could act, and he glowed with youthful vulnerability and sex appeal. You could almost peel it off the screen.

By now, MCA was acting as Sinatra's agent and Dorsey had finally agreed to accept $60,000 to sever his ties with Frank once and for all. Whilst the star did what he did best, sing and pull the girls, his media machine whirled and twisted around him. Now, at the end of 1943, he had become his own dream; a superstar the equal of Crosby or Valentino, a singer who had smashed attendance records and won over the wealthy and influential.

When the United States abolished deferments for unmarried fathers, Sinatra submitted to the physical examination for the U.S. Army. His perforated eardrum and being underweight disqualified him for service, as did his emotional instability, as the examiner noted; although that was based on Sinatra's own confession, it must be added. There was also talk of bribery, which turned out to be unsubstantiated. All of this didn't help to quell the calls for the 'wealthy wop' to do something for the country that was making him so much money and fame. And Frank can certainly not have been too delighted at the prospect of leaving his fickle American career on hold, or having it permanently stalled by getting killed. He was accorded 4F status (totally disqualified from service in uniform); American men could be heard adding the words *"draft dodger"* to Sinatra's name. And worse; Sinatra showed little sign of being upset that he would be able to, and did, live it up with the babes whilst the boys were dying away from home. All of this meant that by the war's end, Sinatra was known as *"…The most hated man in the armed services"*.

With the new year of 1944 came the beginning of a new life for Frank Sinatra when he became a legal resident of California, remaining so for the rest of his life. One indication that things were changing was his new show on CBS, "The Frank Sinatra Program", which could be heard for 30 minutes every Wednesday night. There was a new RKO feature film, too, "Step Lively", in which he was joined by Sammy Cahn as the songwriter.

Apart from the armed services, the other thing that was tugging him down as far as he was concerned was family life; on January 10th 1944 his wife Nancy gave birth to a son at 5:50 PM. As with his daughter so with his son; Frank Sinatra the father was absent from the birth, and his son would have no choice but to become accustomed to a life

Opposite page: A young Frank Sinatra making a telephone call on the set of the film 'Step Lively'

without a father to turn to. Frank phoned early the next morning, briefly, to check on the two, mother and son. Later he sang to them on the radio, *"This love of mine goes on and on, tho' life is empty since you have gone"*. Whatever Frank was feeling, Nancy was very lonely; she missed the man she loved, terribly.

Frank couldn't bear to be alone and he filled his life with people and sound, especially from his entourage and other hangers on. George Evans was far more present for Nancy than her own husband, and he began to urge her to move to the West Coast. But Nancy was astute enough to know that she would be even more alone amongst the showbiz crowd, competing with the other women. She was right, who could compete against the likes of Marlene Dietrich or the delectable young Ava Gardner, whose meetings with Frank, although platonic, had become more frequent. And this world was about to expand even more.

Louis B. Mayer had seen him sing, and within months a five-year contract had been hammered out between Frank's lawyers and Metro-Goldwyn-Mayer's lawyers that would see Sinatra take home $260,000 per year, make one non-Metro-Goldwyn-Mayer film per year, and included sixteen guest appearances on radio, plus publishing rights to the music in every second film. The RKO contract bit the dust, as had the one with Dorsey. He was now a protégé of MCA, whose legal team did the necessary squeezing. For Sinatra, only the best was good enough. Yet, George Evans knew that the train could be derailed in a moment and the best way to prevent that happening was to have the Sinatra family united in California. Frank, also, was finally persuaded that this would be the best move, and while he was back east for his son's christening, he invited Nancy and the children to come and join him out west. He promised her the moon in a Cadillac; she hoped; but deep in her heart, she knew.

Early in 1944, the family went by train to Los Angeles, finally coming to rest at a house with pink stucco that once belonged to Mary Astor on 10051 Valley Spring Lane, hidden behind a wall to keep anyone from getting close enough to touch him, and a stone's throw from Bob Hope's house. Sinatra hadn't seen the pink house before he moved in. For the kids, contact with Hollywood life, sailing and kayaking in the sunshine made for idyllic days. As for Frank, well, the house was big, which would keep his claustrophobia at bay. He had his own sailboat in which he could play poker with his cronies. His surroundings were expanding to keep pace with his career and his view of himself. The only fly in the ointment was that the press had turned against him, printing vicious articles showing him to be

a carefree hedonist whose life was wine women and song whilst the men of the country were abroad, fighting and dying. And the fact that he earned $840,000 in 1944 didn't make George Evans' job of producing positive publicity for his singer any easier.

As Sinatra mingled with the good, the not so good and the famous at showbiz parties, he met a man who seemed unlikely to become an addition to his Varsity; his name was Peter Lawford, a 21-year-old English contract player, far below Sinatra's status. But they both seemed to recognise an affinity in the other. Indeed, so it turned out to be; overbearing mothers, slight physical imperfections Lawford's right arm had become slightly deformed when he fell into a glass door as a child a complex character. He was six-foot tall and incredibly handsome. And he had humour. It was the start of a long friendship.

Now it was time for Sinatra to win over a sceptical Hollywood and persuade the doubters that this singer had what it took to become a real star in Tinseltown. His first film was going to be "Anchors Away",

Left: George Murphy (3rd from right), Frank Sinatra and Gloria DeHaven (2nd from right) appear in a scene from the movie 'Step Lively'

Right: Marlene Dietrich

in which he would be partnered with Gene Kelly, who taught Frank a few dance steps. By all accounts that was more than enough, because with Frank's dance style, any more might have put the other dancers out of action. Nancy Sinatra tells the story that Pamela Britton, who was playing a waitress in the film, said to Frank after he had trodden on her toes, *"Oh that's all right. You're very light on my feet".*

Frank's abrupt character, borne aloft by impatience, fear and a lack of grounded self-confidence in his own talent, engendered his sharp tone, so that *"one take Charlie"*, his nickname because he hated doing more than one take, became no one's favourite mate. On top of that, his embarrassment flung him into depression. When his insecurity finally drove him to ask to see the rushes, something not done in Hollywood but which he was given permission to do, it almost ended his Hollywood career. When he turned up with his entourage and they were forbidden entrance, Sinatra blew a gasket and walked off the picture, wisely returning next day. He then let loose in an interview saying, *"... pictures stink and most of the people in them do, too. Hollywood won't believe I'm through, but they'll find out I mean it."* Sinatra was becoming showbiz royalty and at the same time a royal pain in the backside. His team went into overdrive with damage limitation and Sinatra stayed in Hollywood.

Still, Frank Sinatra was just one glimmer in the overwhelming glamour in Hollywood, but he was the undisputed king on the east coast; he travelled back there once the film with Gene Kelly had finished, reading on the train, filling in the gaps in his knowledge that stung him when he met more educated people. It was the denigration of Italian Americans that made him a champion of those at the same end of the racial discrimination whip, especially the black community, and his reading brought him up to scratch on the current situation in America. In fact, Sinatra, that man of contradictions, had a soft heart when he allowed it the freedom to breathe. He could never countenance black musicians being at the wrong end of a racist stick, as Sammy Davis Jr. would discover. He had a penchant for black women and planted a proper kiss on Billie Holiday's lips. And he could also be a compassionate humanitarian when his emotional pendulum swung in the right direction, allowing him to forget, or perhaps polish, his own ego. He bravely went to sing and talk in Gary, a tough steel-producing town in Indiana, where white students had walked out of their school when the principal had allowed 270 black students to use the orchestra and the swimming pool and join in the classes. There were no incidences at his concert; neither was there any change in the town's attitudes, but Sinatra gained cachet for his efforts, and his moral stature rose. A 15-minute movie called "The House I Live in", in which Sinatra played himself, showed Sinatra in the role of philosophical adviser and

Left: Gene Kelly and Frank Sinatra comment on some pin-ups to their shipmates in a scene from MGM's 'Anchors Aweigh', directed by George Sidney

compassionate, strong, yet understanding man, and this cemented the image that Evans wanted of his client. The film made Sinatra the darling of the left of the political spectrum.

It was during this summer that a man came into Sinatra's life tangentially, who would be an enormously influential friend for as long as he lived. Unable to sing at a gig in Manhattan, Sinatra was replaced by a young, tall and handsome 27-year-old singer from Ohio, whose real name was Dino Crocetti. He sounded like Sinatra and sang the same songs; his stage name was Dean Martin.

Having met his hero President Franklin D. Roosevelt, to whom he had donated major campaign funds, and after promoting the purchase of war bonds, Frank was back on stage at the Paramount in New York in October. There was a riot in the streets outside when many of the young fans were turned away because those inside refused to give up their seats for the next performances. 441 patrolmen and women were needed to keep order. Frank sang for 45 minutes and did six shows, whilst outside on the street there was hysteria and girls fainted. The day would be remembered in history as the Columbus Day Riot. Dean Martin and Jerry Lewis would get the same treatment just five years later.

Then it was off to the recording studio for nineteen songs to be recorded with Alex Stordahl, the orchestrator. Amongst them was "Saturday Night (Is the Loneliest Night of the Week)".

Tales of Sinatra's uncontrollable temperament and lavishly roisterous life style were also beginning to seep through George Evans's firewall. The results would eventually rear up to bite Sinatra. It was difficult to keep the stream of Frank's lovers out of the headlines and now Frank felt he was deeply in love with a girl named Marilyn Maxwell, likewise a singer. Whereas the other girls were in and out like yoyos, Marilyn was a recurring theme in his life. He had no home life to speak of; there were various members of the Barbato family in residence at any one time in his house, which irked him intensely. Nancy and he seemed to be permanently arguing, even during the odd moments when they were together and alone. What made it worse was that he knew she still loved him despite all that he was doing.

The showbiz papers followed his tracks and regaled their readers with his antics and his revolving roster of girlfriends. The singer pirouetted between the east and west coasts, drinking in the nightlife, talking, working, staying out late, escorting women home. It was a life in the fast lane. Nancy reaped one reward, at least, from Frank's womanising; Lana Turner had become her friend, enjoyed talking to this down-to-earth woman, and was glad to escape the bitching women and unreliable men of Hollywood for a while, in the pink stuccoed house.

Right: Frank Sinatra relaxing in his dressing room at the Paramount Theater. 1945

Fly Me to the Moon

Fly Me to the Moon

Left: Bobby Soxers waiting in line outside the Paramount Theatre

Above: Crowds wait in front of the Paramount Theatre before a Frank Sinatra performance, New York City, October 21, 1944

A Sinatra Inside an Enigma

Sinatra entered what turned out to be the prolific year of 1945 without a new contract for the Lucky Strike "Your Hit Parade". But there was plenty to do in the recording studio, where he spent at least one recording session every month throughout the year. Forty-three sides made it to the presses and four of those made it to the top 10. Amongst the songs was "Put Your Dreams Away", which then became his theme song. His voice was strong in Latin-gospel numbers, schmaltzy ballads and timeless rhythms. One song that year which became a big Sinatra hit was known as "Nancy (with the Laughing Face)", which Sinatra gave to his daughter Nancy for her 4th birthday. Phil Silvers had produced the lyrics at a party and Jimmy Van Heusen had composed the tune.

President Roosevelt died in April and Sinatra felt deep sorrow, along with most of the rest of the USA. And then World War II ended. Evans thought a post-VE day tour by Frank would be a good idea.

Why hadn't he gone to entertain the troops before? Contrary to the impression that the FBI had prevented him from getting a visa because of his left-wing activities, the FBI showed no real interest in Sinatra until after the war, when his political activities, amongst other things, aroused their suspicions. Perhaps, as one commentator mentioned, the simple truth was that Frank Sinatra was frightened of going to Europe during wartime.

The tour was arranged, however, and with Phil Silvers the brilliant comic cleverly 'bullying' Sinatra before he sang, so that the GIs could vicariously get their own back on the "draft dodger", the tour through the dusty GI camps was a great success.

So, too, was the film "Anchors Aweigh" that was released in June.

Now, however, it was not the girls Sinatra needed to worry about; although he didn't know it, by the end of 1945 the FBI had trained their sights on "Frank Sinatra, well-known radio and movie star". He was suspected of being a member of the Communist Party. Without a war to concentrate on, the country's conservatives needed a focus for their fears about their country, and they found it in the House Un-American Activities Committee. That was just the warm-up show, however; the FBI would have their work cut out investigating Frank's other connections; those that put him side by side with the mob and gangsters.

It is now widespread knowledge that if you were an entertainer between the 1930s and 1960s you would come into contact with the members of the criminal underworld in America simply because most of the clubs and nightclubs were owned and operated by the mob. Frank Sinatra swam in and out of these shark-infested waters like a pro and no one could ever pin him down in any aspect of his life or dealings with the characters that peopled the underworld. By the time Sinatra arrived in Hollywood, Benny "Bugsy" Siegel was already ensconced in the celluloid goldmine, a mobster who carried a halo of danger around with him like a union badge. He was also handsome, blue-eyed and well dressed. When Frank Sinatra met him, what did the singer see? Another self-made man who had pushed through the odds stacked up against him to get the top of his profession? Another outsider, another man with special talents? Whatever it was, Sinatra fell under Siegel's spell and would talk openly about Siegel's 'hits' as though they were the latest football scores, describing the methods used for elimination as though they were harmless football

Above: Mugshot of Benny "Bugsy" Siegel

Opposite page: Portrait of Frank in 1945

techniques. In truth, Frank was filled with admiration and awe for his new 'friend'. Perhaps Frank saw himself in that role if life had taken him along a different path. He would certainly have displayed the necessary ruthlessness; even at the beginning of his career he never let friendship or personal relationships stand in the way of his ambition. His career was sacrosanct, and even Manie Sacks, who thought of himself as a close friend, was soon led to realise that either you did things the way Sinatra wanted and to Sinatra's advantage, or you were yesterday's news.

Not that Sinatra had everything his own way; Harry James and Bing Crosby were still keeping him below them in the Billboard charts, and the luscious Ava Gardner had married Artie Shaw; and begun to drink. She would not enter Sinatra's life in a big way for some time yet.

Ever aware of his educational shortcomings, Sinatra was keen to give himself musical credence, and he persuaded Manie to let him conduct an orchestra playing the music of a classical and popular music composer, Alec Wilder. The result was "Frank Sinatra Conducts the Music of Alec Wilder". Sinatra couldn't read a note of music and, of course, the musicians could have played together blindfolded. Nonetheless, his association with classical musicians gave him kudos in the world at large and helped in part to allay any residual feelings of inadequacy he may have harboured. And the general consensus was that his love of the music and his innate musicality gave him a true ability to be a conductor.

Post-war America was changing its musical tastes. For a singer, the mantra was 'change or vanish' and Sinatra was not about to do that. Ironically, Artie Shaw was extending his career by lavishly orchestrating some of the old songs that had become passé, and he pointed the way for Sinatra, too. The two musicians would become rivals in more ways than one. But that year of 1946 was going to be an intense recording year for Sinatra and he sang 57 songs into the studio microphones, amongst them, "That Old Black Magic", "Begin the Beguine" and "The Girl That I Marry". In March, he released "The Voice of Frank Sinatra", proving that he was not sitting on his laurels. It was issued as a four record box set and was, perhaps, the first concept album, having a common thread running through all the songs. It was an instant success; it was Sinatra at his confident, seductive and technical best. It hit number 1 on the Billboard chart and stayed there for seven weeks. America old and young had fallen under the spell of a singer who had found his own road, his own inimitable style. As he began to climb the charts, another award came his way; it was a special Academy Award for "The House I Live in".

Right: Kathryn Grayson talks to Frank Sinatra and Jimmy Durante in a scene from the film 'It Happened In Brooklyn', 1947

Frank's restless nature was given sustenance with a cross-country tour in late March, and he filled the rest of the summer with concerts in venues between San Francisco and New York. Audience numbers swelled as **The Voice** album climbed the charts; 10,000 came to see him in Philadelphia. People swarmed into the 25,000-seat venue, Madison Square Garden. Then there was work for a new film, "It Happened in Brooklyn".

Sinatra was at the peak of his popularity, but if anything, the pressures were even greater and fed his neuroses, with the consequence that his anxiety and panic attacks during filming would see him simply leave the set or not even show up for the day's shoot. Still, there was always the delicious Marilyn Maxwell to soothe his nerves. Which she did superbly. George Evans did his absolute best to keep her in the background and his client's image clean. It was a losing battle; Marilyn might become history, but there would always be an immediate replacement. Even before Marilyn exited stage left, there already was one. Frank was infatuated with her. The luscious Lana Turner.

His broad smile when they were photographed dancing almost cheek to cheek together in the summer of 1946 said it all. Turner's visits to Nancy were curtailed, of course. Poor Nancy. The train was running too fast, now, no one could control it; the driver least of all; Frank.

Frank Sinatra never wanted to be alone. And if it wasn't girls, it was shady characters, as the FBI noted. During the summer, the Fischetti's, first cousins to Al Capone, were being associated with Sinatra's name after the singer had reserved them deluxe suites at the Waldorf Hotel in New York. What was wrong with that innocent favour?

As summer passed into autumn, there was an opportunity for another side of Frank Sinatra to come to the fore. Phil Silvers was planning a double act at the Copacabana in New York with his friend Rags Ragland. Just three days short of his 41st birthday on August the 20th, Rags died unexpectedly. Silvers needed a stooge for his act, and the Copacabana could make a career. If he cancelled the gig he would never play there again, that was made very plain to him. In fact, cancelling could very well crash his career altogether. Silvers was desperate. He phoned Sinatra again and again pleading with him to stand in for Rags. Even though Silvers had helped Sinatra out during the tour of army bases at the end of World War II, Sinatra didn't take kindly to being asked to reciprocate any favours or acts of kindness he had benefited from. He refused, saying that he couldn't leave the picture he was working on. True, he was sincerely worried about upsetting L. B. Mayer by leaving the film set yet again. There was nothing else for it; Silvers went on alone at the Copacabana.

The first part of his act went down like uncooked ravioli. In his dressing room during a break, Silvers mused on the lost opportunity, and the detrimental effect this could all have on his career.

And then the door opened.

Frank had come to the rescue.

They went on together, repeated their army act and brought the house down. It was the glorious side that could counterbalance the self-centred character that was Frank Sinatra. Exhausted, Frank didn't turn up on the set of his film for several days afterwards.

There was another reason for his exhaustion, though.

Frank was Nancy's partner on paper only by this stage. His

mind and body were elsewhere. Nancy knew this, but hope is hard to deflate. The situation began to seriously bubble shortly after she found a diamond bracelet in the glove compartment of his car. She assumed it was a present for her, but it soon found its way onto the wrist of Marilyn Maxwell. When Nancy saw it there, she almost fainted with the shock. Suffice it to say, Maxwell was soon out of the house, and Sinatra was trying to placate his wife by saying Marilyn meant nothing to him.

Nancy might have been forgiven for exhibiting a little cynicism.

But, of course, Marilyn was heading for the exit anyway because Lana was on the menu. She had been the cause of Frank phoning Nancy in October to ask for a separation, and not even the urgings of George Evans could change his mind. He disappeared from the set of the movie he was working on and went to Palm Springs. With Lana Turner. And it was there that Sinatra met Ava Gardner once more, on the arm of Howard Hughes, this time. Inevitably they found

Far Left: Lana Turner

Bottom Left: Al Capone, who was the Fischetti's first cousin

Top Right: Modern Times issue where Frank was voted Man Of The Year

A Sinatra Inside an Enigma

Above: Sinatra poses for a portrait to promote his NBC Radio show, 1946 in New York City

Opposite page: American comedian Phil Silvers and Frank in fancy dress costumes for a New Year's Eve party, 31st December 1947

Next Page: Sinatra and musicians in studio during recording session at CBS, 1947

themselves dancing together. Closely.

Back in Hollywood, Frank was presented with the Modern Screen Magazine award for Most Popular Star of 1946. But the pressure to get back with his family began to build on all sides, from the press and from Louis B. Mayer. George Evans worked overtime to limit the damage. Even Frank couldn't resist, and after an opening night for Phil Silvers on Beverly Boulevard, he and Nancy danced, went out into the night, ended up in his apartment, and got to work increasing the numbers in their family.

For a while he focused a little more attention on his family. There were presents, with photographers at hand, of course, when he got together with them. But the work, his career, made these occasions extremely rare. The kids mostly only heard their father, they hardly ever saw him. It wasn't just the professional commitments; Lana was working in town.

Frank hadn't turned a personal corner, and before long he was in trouble with Mayer again for making unauthorised radio appearances. The press homed in eagerly on Sinatra the bad boy. Frank gave them plenty of reasons to see him as that. He made himself work constantly to stay in the public consciousness and the strain of wanting to remain at the top, believing himself to be the best and therefore not like other mortals, made him lash out, making him more enemies than friends. Not even his fans were spared; he once banned anyone under 21 from his radio broadcasts. In December 1946, Sinatra was voted the *"least cooperative star"* of the year by the Hollywood Women's Press Club.

But what did he care, because at his New Year's Eve party, Peter Lawford arrived with his date. She had just turned 24 and become a major star in the film The Killers, with Burt Lancaster. She was bursting with youthful energy and confidence. And she was stunningly beautiful. Frank had admired those looks before. It was Ava Gardner.

She, like Frank, couldn't bear to be alone. That night, they weren't destined to be. Her presence, however, on the threshold to 1947, seemed like an omen for the future. But first, 1947 had more serious problems to offer the singer.

Nancy decided to have an abortion.

Sinatra was now carrying a gun, which was probably not destined to protect the dollar rolls that he always carried around with him, however many thousands of notes there might be. A trip early in the New Year to Miami and Cuba in the company of various Fischettis would explain that firearm more easily. Frank, it seems, was more attracted to and more involved in the underworld lifestyle than he would have others believe. But it is hard to believe that Sinatra was

naive in going on this trip, carrying, incidentally, a heavy suitcase containing... *"… painting oils and jewellery"*; an odd thing for a star to do at any time, let alone Frank Sinatra. Or that he accidentally happened to be in Havana for what one columnist described as *"… a sort of hoodlums' summit with the big names of the mob"*. Anyone who was anyone in the underworld seemed to be present, from Lucky Luciano and Frank Costello to the Fischettis and Joe Adonis. Sinatra, staying on the floor below Luciano, literally rubbed shoulders with them all for four days. His protestations of innocence, of course, echoed those he gave to Nancy. It is hardly surprising that the fluff stuck to his jacket, so to speak.

It was Nancy's turn to strike back. Frank had suggested a Valentine break in Acapulco. When he eventually arrived there, he discovered that Nancy had been true to her word.

She had gone through with the abortion.

This act of defiance and independence cannot have sat well in Sinatra's world, where everything and everyone was neatly labelled according to Frank's taste, and found good if it stayed there unchallenging and tame. His daughter Nancy played down this sad event and reduced it to the flare of a match flame. According to her, Sinatra then tried very hard to improve his behaviour and attended to his wife more closely, once more. That would never be easy. But he did want a new house for Nancy. He was sincere, too. Underneath the crazy paving life he led, Sinatra had the heart, dusted, perhaps, with an Italian sense of possessiveness, but just not the willpower, to be a good husband.

By October of 1947, Nancy was pregnant again.

The new house would be called Twin Palms and would be built in Palm Springs with a swimming pool in the shape of a grand piano. It was Sinatra's desert retreat. It might also help to quell the gossip column inches that constantly told readers that he was about to leave his wife for good. When it was finished in 1948, far from becoming a refuge, it seemed to become simply another place for Frank to continue as before, away from prying eyes. Pregnant wife or not.

After the Havana incident, Frank was also in Mayer's black books again and was called in to see the great man for a verbal coldwater session. Mayer was loaning him to RKO, and to play... a priest! The effect of Mayer's punishment on the singer, no doubt, was to leave him feeling humiliated and resentful.

Right: Frank holds on to his five-year-old son, Frank Jr., who prepares to jump off a diving board into a swimming pool, California

Buddy Can You Spare a Dime?

There was good news at least in April 1947 with the release of "It Happened in Brooklyn" in which Sinatra starred with Kathryn Grayson and Jimmy Durante. There was a lot of praise for Sinatra's performance and his singing abilities, which were shown to their fullest in the song "Time After Time". "Sinatra becomes a smoother performer every time out" was the opinion of the Newsweek reporter. Nonetheless, the film wasn't a success and lost the company $138,000.

Any good news, however, was sandwiched tightly in between bad, and the negative headlines were filtering through more than anyone cared to see; also, the anti-Sinatra Brigade were sharpening their knives and closing in on his reputation. Frank helped them whenever he could. One night in April he went into Ciro's on Sunset Boulevard. The journalist Lee Mortimer, who'd had his verbal knives in Sinatra's back for some time, was dining there. Having finished eating, he was standing outside, so the story goes, when Sinatra came from behind him and punched him behind the ear with his right fist. Mortimer was knocked to the ground. And there, apparently, he was held down by a large man in a pinstriped suit, whereupon Sinatra began to pummel and swear at the prostrate journalist. Rather ineffectually, it would seem. A photographer intervened, and Sinatra, honour satisfied, went back inside. Mortimer got up, more angry than hurt.

The incident might have slipped quietly away, even though Mortimer lodged a complaint to the police about the incident. Unfortunately, Sinatra decided to go on the offensive with the press and ended up telling a convoluted story marbled with lies and self-

pity, and accused the journalist of calling him *"a dago son of a bitch"*. The knives from the Hearst press flashed mercilessly. Frank found himself contrite in front of Louis B. Mayer once more, and the mogul forced his star to issue a statement which basically said that he had been lying about Mortimer and regretted the incident. Mayer also insisted that Sinatra pay the writer a $9000 settlement. It should have been a non event, even as an indication of the sidetrack that Sinatra's emotional life and character had disappeared along there was a lifelong conflict between the singer's desire to be a tough guy, yet knowing he wasn't; of having to live out that toughness vicariously by using the ruthlessness of others. The consequences of that for his ego were all negative instead, the spat was a trigger for an assault on the singer's character. Sinatra was dropped from the radio show Old Gold. Nor was Mortimer prepared to let bygones be bygones. He went to Edgar Hoover to accuse Sinatra of having connections with the Mafia; claiming, for example, that a gangster named Willie Moretti had apparently backed Sinatra in the early days. The Fischettis also appeared in Mortimer's report.

Frank's FBI file was growing apace.

In June, Bugsy Siegel was eating at a restaurant called Jack's when a bullet took him out of the game permanently. The hit was a result of the Havana Mafia conference, instigated by Charlie Fischetti, planned by a man named Frankie Carbo, who, it was said, might have *"helped"* Tommy Dorsey to understand how good it would be for his health to let Frank Sinatra move on.

And perhaps the irony wasn't missed when Sinatra received the Thomas Jefferson Award for fighting intolerance on April the 13th. Sinatra truly liked black people and employed black entertainers in his concerts whenever he could. He was also aware of his indebtedness to people like Billie Holiday who had shown him the direction to go as a singer. One man who benefited most from Sinatra's goodwill, of course, was the extraordinarily talented Sammy Davis Jr. They became friends in 1941, and the very young Sammy Davis and his family had appeared with the Tommy Dorsey Orchestra.

Into this dangerous mix, another destabilising element had been introduced; a man named Joseph McCarthy had begun his investigations into suspected Communists and Communist organisations. And what was Frank doing? He was chomping at the bit, spending his days in glued-on hair (in later films his ears would be taped back) in a film called "The Kissing Bandit". Kathryn Grayson co-starred, and she oozed about as much joy in Frank's love interest as a cat in a dog show. And vice versa.

Right: On horseback listening to J Carrol Naish in a scene from the film 'The Kissing Bandit', 1948

Frank would need all his bravado and inner confidence now. Times were changing; his record sales were declining, as were bookings for his concerts and nightclub gigs, which translated into his income dropping below the $1 million mark for the first time in five years. His agents had to fight to get him another radio show, Your Hit Parade, alongside Doris Day, and he might have been forgiven for wishing they hadn't when one review stated, *"... Frank sounds worse... than he ever has since he first became famous"*.

The Hearst newspapers were in full flow, pouring every sin they could dig up, and even ones they couldn't, over Sinatra's head; the *"sex offence"* of his early years, his underworld connections, draft dodging, and perhaps worst of all at that moment in time, hinting at Communist inclinations. Under this onslaught, receiving the key to Hoboken from the mayor in October for "Frank Sinatra Day" was little consolation.

That the wheel had come off Sinatra's wagon could no longer be denied when Sinatra returned to the scene of his former triumphs with the Hoboken Four, the Capital Theatre, in November and December 1947. The takings were woeful. The adverse publicity was having a devastating effect on Sinatra's career, and the competition, Perry Como for one, had moved in ahead of Sinatra. Yet, Sinatra showed his liberal and sympathetic side at those shows when he hired Sammy Davis Jr. and his family to appear at his concerts. He introduced him as a *"personal friend of mine"*, a brave thing to do in racially riven 1940s America. Davis idolised Sinatra and Sinatra proved to be far more than just a fair-weather friend.

Now that he had made his wife pregnant, he lost interest in her once more, and with his career sliding, he was ripe for something or someone to buoy him up. He had finished his 'punishment' role, the priest in "The Miracle of the Bells", and he wasn't due to start on a Gene Kelly musical, "Take Me Out to the Ballgame", until July 1948. Dangerously, he found himself under occupied. It was time for a legendary partnership to take place. And it was Sammy Cahn's doing.

Frank and Sammy were sharing drinks one night looking down at Sunset Strip from Sinatra's penthouse. Sammy mentioned to Sinatra that if you looked across the street to a row of little houses, you could see one that was occupied by Ava Gardner. Sinatra is said to have shaken his head at this news before putting his hands to his mouth and shouting, *"Ava Gardner!"*

He kept shouting. "We know you're down there, Ava!"

A curtain was drawn back, the window opened, Ava's beautiful head appeared and she waved.

Right: Sinatra as Father Paul and Fred MacMurray (Bill, second from left), in the film 'The Miracle of the Bells', Pennsylvania, USA, 1948

Sinatra took to walking the street outside Ava's house. The inevitable meeting led to a *"Why don't we have drinks and dinner tonight?"* She knew he was married, she knew what he wanted, she thought he was handsome and fun; she accepted the invitation. For once, Sinatra had bitten off more than he could chew. Ava had learned her lessons, she had suffered enough bullying as Mrs. Artie Shaw to last a lifetime, she wasn't about to let Sinatra, much as she was attracted to him, treat her the same way without hitting back.

They ended up in an apartment in which Sinatra tried twice to make her succumb and twice failed. But her kisses worked their wonders on him; he was smitten, even though it was quite some time before they saw each other again.

Their meeting was a spot of warm light in an otherwise cool year of 1948. The Miracle of the Bells was released to general disparagement and Frank's cameo in Till the Clouds Roll By, was dubbed by Hedda Hopper as *"... The worst single moment in a movie ever"*. He did some sporadic radio appearances and managed just eleven recording sessions during the entire year. He was feeling humiliated, and compensated with spoilt brat behaviour. On the 20th of June, the new addition to the family arrived; Tina. Sinatra had taken as much time off as was necessary to drive his wife to the hospital, before he returned to continue his game of charades with friends. He was just a *"picture in the newspaper"* his daughter Nancy said later. There was no indication that that was about to change for Tina.

Sinatra's year dragged on. At one point he found himself singing the cartoon Woody Woodpecker Song. How much worse could it get? It was better not to ask.

Filming began on Take Me Out to the Ballgame, and an embittered Sinatra resorted to his usual childish behaviour of showing up late, wasting time, being unprepared for his scenes. When Louis B. wanted him for a private function, Sinatra agreed and then on the day, left the MGM lot hiding under some boxes in a pickup truck and couldn't be found. His punishment would be another film with RKO, starring Groucho Marx.

Sinatra continued his carousing; there was little work to distract him from it. And then, at a party at David O. Selznick's house, the matchstick and the dynamite got together. He met Ava again. They drank, they fell in love. They went for a drive with some Beefeater gin for company.

Maybe they did drive through town unloading their handguns at anything made of glass and hitting an unfortunate passerby at the same time. Maybe they did end up in the police station and Jack Keller had to fly tens of thousands of dollars into town to keep the tin hat on everything. The legend says they did. Only Jack Keller said it never happened. Whatever took place that night, the world had turned upside down and would never be the same again. Frank loved her as he had never loved anyone, it was overwhelming, and she, too, felt that she had met her soul mate.

Not long after that meeting, they made love, and in Ava's words, *"We became lovers forever - eternally"*. (Many years later, Mia Farrow's *"We never really split up"*, echoed Ava's sentiments.) As lovers, Ava and he may have sizzled, but as companions they would prove to be dramatically incompatible.

Frank's dismal year, with the exception of Ava, began to drag it's ragged frame to the finishing line with a Sinatra Christmas album issued by Columbia in October that faded after just one week in the charts, topping out at number 7, followed by the opening of The Kissing Bandit in November to predictably derogatory reviews. Five years would pass before Sinatra made another album. His second 'punishment' film, It's Only Money, went into production that month. It was no different than any other film, with Sinatra showing up late and not knowing his lines; behaviour which did not endear him to the much more professional Groucho Marx. Jane Russell was also in the film; despite her gorgeous curvature there was, in her words, *"... no funny business at all"*.

The film was a dead duck.

Sinatra began to have vocal problems. He was knocked off the Best Male Singer spot where he had reigned since 1943. He owed taxes. He distracted himself by moving house to live where Loretta Young, Walt Disney and Humphrey Bogart resided, and spent $250,000 to do so. His relationships with his musical collaborators were not working as they had once done. His relationship with his wife had died and been buried long before; a sad Nancy had finally accepted this, too. He had lost confidence in himself for the first time, and in December he told Manie Sacks that he thought his career was over. He was drinking a lot, often drunk, and even with Ava on the scene, unable to leave even a married woman un-pursued. It was, indeed, a low point in the singer's life. Even the rock in Sinatra's raging sea, George Evans, had lost hope in his charge. Evans still fielded the angry phone calls, listening when Frank yelled at him; took the fury head on when he told Frank that Ava Gardner was bad, bad news, she was a hedonist who cared not a wit for what anyone thought. Sinatra decided that he had no more use for the non-compliant Evans.

In March, Take me Out to the Ball Game was released and failed to set the world on fire. Soon, he was filming with Gene Kelly again in **On the Town**. This time Gene Kelly was the headline star. The strain of Frank's failing career was telling on his face. He hit a retired businessman at a party in Palm Springs and the album Frankly Sentimental, didn't make the charts at all; his singles never got higher than number 6, never challenged the king of the moment, Perry Como. His debts were raging

Right: Jules Munshin, Frank Sinatra and Gene Kelly on the Brooklyn Bridge, in a still from Stanley Donen and Gene Kelly's film 'On the Town', New York City

uncontrolled, and by the autumn of 1949 he was doing a five nights a week show for NBC at a much reduced fee. The one beacon of light was the success of On the Town with Gene Kelly, which received great reviews and *"grossed as much in one day in any theatre anywhere"*, as any other motion picture ever, according to one headline. But for Frank there was no real joy, as he had been reduced to second fiddle by Gene Kelly and all of the important ballads had been sung by his rival. It was Gene's success.

Something or someone was going to collapse.

What collapsed, was Sinatra's marriage.

As 1949 had slid into 1950, Frank and Ava had continued their liaison. They were perfect for each other, they were poison for each other. They were temperamentally explosive, they were easily bored and restless, they feared loneliness more than anything, they craved the drink and cigarettes, sex and companionship that their loneliness voraciously demanded in order to remain in its cage.

"You are all I want" Frank told her, but as their relationship progressed,

it was clear that Ava was never going to make him happy. She wanted more than it was possible to give. She lashed him with her tongue, she tormented him with her luxurious femininity. Lacking any sense of limitation she was frightening, it made her unpredictable; made her magnetic. That behavioural template had been set up by Dolly, and Frank was a man on a hook, fiercely attracted and unable to avoid the vortex of her mighty instability. She was madly jealous of him, and yet she held all the cards. Together, they howled at the boredom of normality, the illiberality of the world, and they lived out their uninhibited version of life whenever and wherever they were; there were no rehearsals with this script. Ava demanded all or nothing from Sinatra, divorce or her freedom, and drove him crazy with proving how easy it was for her to get men, by being seen with a minor gangster one day or Robert Mitchum the next. Anger flared, objects flew; they chased one another until they finally once again gave in to their physical desire for one another. This was life as it should be lived, no suburban marriage could survive the scalding heat of such a relationship. Nothing else mattered to Frank and the little bit of work that filtered through was dashed off half-heartedly.

Sinatra knew only one way out and he confided to George Evans that he wanted to marry Ava. The ever-loyal publicist Evans picked up the reigns once more, once he had agreed to do battle. Yet he never got the chance to prove his loyalty that was so vital to Frank's survival, just one last time. George Evans died of a massive coronary on the 27th of January 1950 aged just 48. Frank knew just how much he owed this man, and he put Philip Evans, George's son, onto his payroll for life.

Nancy and Frank had fierce rows; as usual he tried to lie his way to peace, until she no longer had the strength to carry on the charade. She decided that she wanted to end it. She knew about Ava, of course she did, she knew about all of Frank's dalliances. In one final row, she threw some of his clothes out of the window and he walked out.

Now he was openly seen in public with Ava. Nancy changed the locks on their home two days after their eleventh wedding anniversary. Their fraught marriage was over. In February 1950, she let the world know that they were splitting up; not divorcing, she was a Catholic.

The floodgates opened in front of Ava Gardner, and the contorted hate mail came flushing in from nuns, Catholic priests, students and, of course, the press, who referred to her as *"Bitch-Jezebel-Gardner"*. In moralistic America, the duo had sunk to the bottom of the cesspit, which meant that it was open hunting season for the 'press gangs'. For two such sensitive and vulnerable characters, none of this passed them by leaving them unaffected. Frank was getting heartbreaking phone calls from his daughter and was taking pills to go to sleep, to wake up, to relax, washed down with copious quantities of alcohol in

Above: Perry Como

Opposite page: Frank with Ava Gardner

Above: Frank enjoys coffee and donuts in his trailer during a break in filming

Opposite page: Sinatra at Liederkranz Hall, New York

the company of Ava.

Frank had been booked for a series of shows at the Copacabana and was a nervous wreck on the day, even though Ava was there, even though she was supposed to be in England, filming. Their nerves were on edge; Frank's voice was not what it had been, although the shows went well. But Ava was now finding out what kind of company Frank kept, in the form of the Fischetti brothers; and she wasn't happy about it. In fact, she was so unhappy about it that she decided to go and see her ex, Artie Shaw. Shaw had always been scathing about Sinatra, and Sinatra had been stung when Shaw had refused to employ him in the early 40s. This was trouble in the making, and trouble duly stepped up to the line. Everyone involved had a different version of what happened next and all of them were fun to read. Ava stormed out; Frank yelled down the phone that he was going to kill himself. Frank turned up at Shaw's apartment ready for fisticuffs. Ava confessed to Shaw, *"I thought he was a big stud… It's like being in bed with a woman"*. Whether that is true or not, Ava would find herself becoming less sexually satisfied by her *"Francis"*, as she called him.

Acting more like a pouting child, Sinatra had indeed said over the phone, *"I'm going to kill myself - now!"* according to Ava. Then there was a shot that sent her into complete shock. When she rushed over to Frank's room, she discovered that he had fired a gun into a pillow and mattress. So then the desk clerk phoned, the mattress had to be dispensed with, the police arrived and the story hit the papers in one form or another. All in a day's work for Mr. Sinatra.

But in April, Sinatra was tired and he started coughing up blood; he lost his voice entirely in the middle of a show. It was terrifying. He had a persistent cough. He could hardly get through a recording session, so that in the end, the musicians would have to record the background tracks and Sinatra would return later to add the vocals. Sinatra was bouncing along the ground.

None of this, however, was as bad as the news about Ava, now filming in Spain, who was apparently in a liaison with a bullfighter. Frank compensated, or got revenge, with Marilyn Maxwell and also… well, did it matter with whom else? He obsessed about Ava, telephoning her, sending off cables, hardly able to communicate over the crackling and faint transatlantic lines that infuriated him and made his longing even worse.

Nothing was going right. And then in February came another blow. Having made a joke about Louis B. Mayer and his mistress that reached the ears of the mighty man, Mayer decided that he, too, had wearied of the relationship with Sinatra and sacked him, with the words, *"I want you to leave and I don't ever want you to come back again"*.

At the end of April, Nancy was in court having filed for maintenance from Sinatra. She also asked for the custody of the three children on the grounds of *"extreme cruelty"* and *"grievous mental suffering"*. His income

Right: Sinatra looking good in his trademark Fedora

was estimated at $934,740 for 1949.

Manie Sacks had now departed from Columbia and Sinatra was being pushed relentlessly by Mitch Miller, who knew that musical tastes had changed and wanted more rhythm in the Sinatra numbers. Joe Public wanted rhythm but not necessarily Sinatra. And Sinatra could not infuse his numbers with life; everything he released fell short of the charts.

Doctors told Frank he needed to rest his vocal chords; okay, so he would rest. He chose Charlie Fischetti's mansion in Miami to get away from it all.

Then he flew to Spain...

... where Ava was having the time of her life with the handsome bullfighter. It didn't take long for the rows to start and the bullfighter to swear that he was going to kill Sinatra. It all made great headlines for the congregating reporters, until Sinatra decided he was going to leave early. So, after a parting worthy of a Hollywood movie ending, he and Van Heusen set off for Paris, where apparently, they consoled themselves with the French ladies of the night. The bullfighter haunted and mocked Sinatra all the way back to America, dripping off the reporters' questions at every turn.

The trip had been one ridiculous faux pas. It certainly hadn't helped his emotional state, as he had returned home to a professional vacuum with hardly any work, apart from an appearance on the Star-Spangled Review, Bob Hope's TV show, for which the comedian had engaged him when no one else wanted to. It wasn't a successful start and the reviews were tepid. Then there was one more week on radio in Light up Time. His contract for the show expired and was not renewed.

There was, at least, one piece of good news; his voice had returned. With it came a mini success; Mitch Miller decided to change the style of Sinatra's offerings to an unwilling public, and with **Good Night Irene** Sinatra got his biggest hit in over three years when it went to number 5 on the Billboard charts. And there was something else to look forward to in July, when he would sing in England at the Palladium in London.

Where Ava, having jettisoned her toreador, was at Shepperton Studios putting the finishing touches to her film.

England was still stuck in the austerity of the post-war years and had never fallen out of love with Frank Sinatra. His reception in Britain echoed those of his early successes in America; the crowds gathered and teenage girls screamed. His confidence surged. He and Ava were happily reunited and he threw himself into rehearsals for his show. It was a rip roaring success. There was mass hysteria of the kind he loved, and the reviewers were full of praise; "... A superb performer and a great artiste". Frank the Voice was still impressive.

Back in America, he was reunited with Ava. They started living together in a beach house in Pacific Palisades. Their personal problems followed them. Ava's sister 'Bappie' disliked Sinatra intensely and told Eva that she thought he was bad for her career. Ava was not best pleased when Frank brought his kids over at weekends. And she let Frank know it. Ava wanted to get married, but now Frank was stalling, using Nancy and her Catholicism and reluctance for a divorce as the excuse. So the roller coaster relationship continued its predictable pattern; arguments, sex, outings; rinse and repeat.

There is an odd footnote to the Sinatra story at this point, when information reached the offices of the FBI to the effect that Frank Sinatra, uncomfortably aware that he was being linked to the mob, wanted to "... do anything, even if it affects his livelihood and costs him his job" and feed information "with respect to subversives" to the FBI. His approaches were anything but welcome in the bureau offices or in the ears of Edgar Hoover. Perhaps it was all intended as a decoy by Sinatra. But not even the FBI wanted anything to do with him.

Later in September, Frank was back in the negative news headlines when Nancy was granted custody of the children and awarded a settlement of one third of his income up to $150,000 and 10% of the next $150,000 for as long as she lived. Even allowing for the bitterness of heartbreak, the Frank Sinatra described by Nancy and her sister was one of a selfish, arrogant and unpleasant man, and unfortunately had all the ring of truth. Nonetheless, their daughter Nancy describes her mother afterwards as crying softly at night away from the children's ears and eyes, deeply hurt and distraught about what had happened.

The next attempt at grinding Frank's career back into movement came in October with The Frank Sinatra Show on CBS Television. The show was fairly insipid, a mixture of Sinatra's songs interspersed with guests ranging from Buster Keaton and Phil Silvers through to Louis Armstrong and Sammy Davis Jr. It managed to remain on air for the next two years. The problem was more with Frank himself than the material. He hated rehearsing and was constantly hours late, took wrong decisions about guests, and generally reverted to his old bullying, tyrannical ways. Producer Irving Mansfield noted that Sinatra washed his hands over and over and over again like Lady Macbeth. A psychologist would have had a field day. His mind, of course, was distracted, chasing Ava in jealous fantasies that erupted into loud anger when he couldn't contact her. Artie Shaw, as usual, was the chief suspect. "I know she's with that bastard. I'll kill her. I'll kill her. I'll kill her."

Destabilised, unable to control the situation, he was spiralling downwards emotionally. His career hobbled forwards like a drunken hobo, and when his first 10-inch LP came out, Sing and Dance with Frank Sinatra, it only ever saw the Billboard charts from a distance.

It's Tough at the Top, but It's Worse at the Bottom

A thankless year came to an end in December with Sinatra being questioned about his connections to the American underworld, by the Special Committee on Organised Crime in Interstate Commerce. The hearings were televised and were it not for Sol Gelb, his attorney, Frank's career might have gone from bad to non-existent, because incriminating photos emerged, such as the one of Frank with his arm around Lucky Luciano, which rather gave the lie to his line of not knowing anyone in the underworld except to say hello and goodbye to them. Thanks to Gelb, Sinatra didn't have to attend the televised hearings; he was interrogated in private, where some unsavoury rumours rose to the surface involving blackmail, prostitution, and rape. The big question that Frank's interrogator asked several times and which always hovered in the air over Frank Sinatra's life was; *"What's your attraction to these people?"*. Frank, of course, never answered that trap of a question.

He followed this nerve-wracking interrogation by meeting up with Ava, who was close to wrapping on her latest film, Showboat, with which she and MGM were delighted. Her star was in the ascendant. Her exuberance did nothing to endear her to her hollowed-out lover, and before long the screaming started, the flying saucers arrived, the doors slammed and love was made. Déjà vu and Groundhog Day, Frank and Ava style.

In February 1951, with his career in tatters around his feet, Sinatra put his head in a gas oven and turned on the gas. He was in Manie Sacks' Hampshire House suite.

Sacks returned later to find Sinatra on the floor.

Crying.

In March he was crying again when the emotions of a song he was recording, "I'm a Fool to Want You" made him break down, and he fled the studio. It was a wonder he didn't break down in tears when Mitchell then suggested he record a novelty song in May entitled "Mamma Will Bark", a duet between a boy dog and a girl dog. Frank had the last say over what he sang but he did this piece of nonsense anyway. With his career where it was, the dogs could hardly have made matters worse. It was humiliating, though. In fact, the song did all right for itself, charting at number 21. That, as Frank knew to his bitter cost, was show business.

Ava was rubbing salt into the wounds at this point, by making herself scarce, angry that Frank wasn't pressing for a divorce. Jammed into a corner and scared that he was going to lose Ava completely, he went to see Nancy on several occasions to try and get her to consent. Finally, his wife jettisoned the wounded hope of every abandoned woman that her husband would return to her, and agreed. For Nancy it was pain, for Frank it was freedom; suddenly, he was walking on air again.

Briefly.

He started work on a film, Meet Danny Wilson, with Shelley Winters. She disliked her co-star intensely; he was irascible and inattentive. The encounter resulted in invective and a crack on the jaw for Frank from Shelley. At one point, Nancy had to intercede with her to return to finish the picture: Frank wouldn't get paid and her children would be, as she put it, *"... out in the street"*. In contrast, during the shoot, Show Boat was released and Ava became the hottest thing since Mount Etna had last erupted. Hollywood was on its knees to her.

He was on his knees in a deep depression and no one was taking any notice.

Sinatra's bitterness manifested itself in even more dangerous behaviour. In October, he apparently drove straight at a photographer one night and struck him with the car, allegedly screaming, *"Next time I'll kill you! I'll kill you!"* He had Ava confess that she had slept with her bullfighter; he flew into rages, they fought, they made up. One night she walked out on him only to be told that he had taken an overdose, so she rushed to his bedside. No attempted suicide, it was Frank reverting to childhood again, getting his way by whatever means he could.

He was good at making up stories, and so he spun another one, a story of harmony, for the press. He was holding Ava's hand whilst he did so; that was all that mattered.

Wasn't it?

▌*Right:* Sinatra at a rehearsal for the Frank Sinatra Show

Perhaps they really needed the almost daily danger of flying books and lamps, the screaming abuse; perhaps these were the only truly real aspects of their unreal, make-believe worlds.

Frank, meanwhile, made his first appearance in Las Vegas in September; six weeks as top of the bill at the Desert Inn. The shows were a big success, selling out night after night. Little did he know then that Las Vegas was to become his home from home and he would be one of its greatest headliners. Into this little bit of sunshine walked another man who would have a great impact on Frank's life. Jimmy Van Heusen was keeping Frank company in the desert and he discovered a piano player working there called Bill Miller, a man, Van Heusen could see immediately, who possessed great talent. Sinatra was looking for a new pianist and the two were introduced. Miller would become Sinatra's greatest accompanist.

Nancy and Frank's divorce proceedings dragged on. Sinatra didn't have enough money to meet the alimony payments, so until he paid her what he owed there would be no divorce. There was nothing for it; he had to borrow the money from Ava. A new settlement was agreed and Nancy applied for an interlocutory decree of divorce, which was granted in late October. On November 1st 1951, Sinatra was given his divorce in Nevada. One tragicomedy had come to an end; he was finally free to marry Ava Gardner. They applied for a marriage license the very next day in Philadelphia.

Another tragicomedy was about to commence.

It began in the few days before the marriage.

Was it really Ava's ex, Howard Hughes, who had someone send Ava a letter detailing Frank's sex acts with the letter writer? Hughes and Sinatra loathed one another and sat at opposite ends of the political spectrum. The effect was catastrophic; Ava threw her engagement ring away and all hell was let loose and remained on the loose for most of that night. It was finally captured and put back in its jar and on the 7th, twenty guests were present when Frank and Ava not before Frank had *"... spent the whole time at the window upstairs screaming at the press"* according to Ava became man and wife. He was Ava's third husband, following Mickey Rooney and Artie Shaw into wedded bliss. Or rather, blisters.

If Ava thought Frank was going to change she only needed to look at the name of their honeymoon hotel in Havana. It was the Nacional where he had stayed during the infamous 'Mafia conference'. And what was in her mind when, as she said later, they had a fight on the very first night in Cuba and she remembered being blind drunk on the edge of the balcony? *"Frank was afraid to go near me... God I was crazy!"* They had started as they would continue.

Below: Ava's ex, Howard Hughes
Opposite page: Sinatra and Ava tie the knot

It's Tough at the Top, but It's Worse at the Bottom

"Mrs. Sinatra is the happiest girl in the world!"

An undiluted Ava statement. Undoubtedly she was, sometimes.

Back in the States, Mr. and Mrs. Sinatra set up house at Twin Palms. Frank, said friends, was insane about her to the point of being subservient. She dominated him sexually, verbally, and at that moment in time, financially. If either gave of themselves to try and resolve matters, and neither did very often, it was Frank; Ava was selfish, as one of her friends said. Ava would do what she wanted.

Frank had little to do professionally at all. Dean Martin and Nat King Cole filled the airwaves and The Frank Sinatra Show was slipping on a downhill slope. At the London Coliseum in December, playing in front of Prince Philip and Prince Elizabeth in a charity concert, his performance was mediocre, with reports that the audience was yawning. On the 25th of the month, Double Dynamite, which had hung around at RKO for three years, was finally released and went down like a lead balloon. Secretly, Sinatra had hopes for Meet Danny Wilson, which was due to be released in February 1952.

Whilst Frank's career seemed to go from worse to worse still, Ava's was rocketing skywards. She had been loaned out to 20th Century Fox for The Snows of Kilimanjaro, a film loosely, very loosely, based on what Hemingway thought was one of his best stories. It was eventually nominated for two Oscars. Sinatra blew a fuse when he found out about the film, put on his best tyrant cape and arrogantly told Ava that she wasn't allowed to do the movie. Bad move. She told him in no uncertain terms what he could do with himself. Meet Danny Wilson was due to premiere on the 26th of March and the emotional tension was making Frank more nervous than usual. Ava did try to have all her scenes shot consecutively so she could finish the shoot faster. When it didn't work out, Frank exploded again over the phone, so she let him have it with all barrels. Freewheeling ego versus neurotic ego; it wasn't a pretty combination.

Then Meet Danny Wilson was released; *"simple and satisfactory entertainment"*, said the New York Times. Frank Sinatra was *"... charming, natural and casual"*. That tepid review was hardly going to pull Frank's career up by its braces. In fact, the film flopped. At about the same time, MCA, one of the biggest agencies in America, decided they no longer wanted him on its books. In April, a TV show that starred Sinatra on CBS TV and was losing money hand over fist, was ditched. In June, Columbia dropped him, no longer willing to carry a man whose records weren't selling well, and who played in movies no one really wanted to see. Even Ava seemed to put the boot in, flirting as though she wasn't married at all. Frank even had to book his own gigs, if and wherever he could find them, from north to south in almost empty venues. Later in the year, even Hoboken would turn against him, booing him and throwing fruit at him. He managed to land two shows to a few hundred tourists in Hawaii. He persuaded Ava to go with him, ignoring the fact that she had been told to go to Mexico for a new film shoot. She went. The studio suspended her. She flew back to the mainland ahead of him, not because of her suspension, but because she and Frank had quarrelled. They quarrelled again one night, when Frank winked at a woman during one of his shows, and already having drunk too much they argued. Frank hit her so hard she was sent flying, fell over a table and hit the floor, bleeding. Ava, in fact, had a miscarriage, as they discovered at the Cedars of Lebanon Hospital later.

Frank was turning into an ugly parody of a man. One way or another his life was going to have to change before something dire happened. One pressing question that any outsider would have asked at this point went unanswered... where were his supposed Mafia 'friends' when he needed them? The club owners... the men with money and unconventional showbiz leverage. If there were connections, then perhaps they felt they had done their bit already and had no use for him now that he was washed up.

If only he had known it then, change was in the wind.

Had he known he might not have hired a publicist to write a long 'mia culpa' piece in Sinatra's name in the American Weekly, an attempt to win back the public's favour. Frank, said one of his former employees, *"... never apologised to anyone in his life"*. Having been forced to go on his knees, the piece rankled with him ever after.

Where was Ava? Forgiven by her studio that happened quickly, she was a major star now and she was sent on her next film assignment, Vaquero, to the foot of the Rockies, where she spent her time drinking with and bedding some of the crew and the director.

She was mobbed at the premiere of The Snows of Kilimanjaro in September, and was due to shoot Mogambo with Clark Gable and Grace Kelly and the legendary John Ford. There was a brief interlude for a resumption of the vitriolic war games with Frank, during which she took off her wedding ring and then lost it, sending Frank into a spin, and then she was in Hollywood, minus Sinatra, partying and bathing in the 'intentions' of Argentine-born actor Fernando Lamas.

Frank was an almost forgotten figure when he cut his last side for Columbia. At least now he had a new agent at the William Morris agency. And he had been sparked into manic activity having read From Here to Eternity, the novel by James Jones. Angelo Maggio was Frank Sinatra under another name and he burned to do the role. He had correctly identified that his life, maybe literally, depended on it, and he fired off telegrams to the production company, Columbia, to the screenwriter, to the producer. He managed to get Harry Cohn, boss of Columbia pictures, on his own to plead his case and offered to do the film for expenses only. And then it was Ava's turn. She invited Cohn's wife over. *"I want you to get Harry to give Frank the Maggio role in From Here to Eternity."* There was more. *"... I'm afraid he'll kill himself... Please, Joan."*

The result was that Ava Gardner was invited over to Mr. Cohn's house for dinner. And, extraordinarily, she went even further. *"I'll give you a free picture if you will just test him."* Love indeed. A stark contrast to Frank's treatment of Mia Farrow in later life. Buried beneath their increasing acrimony, Ava had not lost her innate humanity.

Frank's humanity wasn't given much of a chance to raise its head above the parapet. And the mother of all arguments was just around the corner. It raged from the Pacific Palisades to Palm Springs taking in Lana Turner en route, whose name was used as a stick to clout Ava and who happened to be staying at the Palm Springs house. Paranoid that Turner and Gardner had been laughing at his expense, Frank raged and fumed. It was becoming tediously predictable, and the two protagonists were adept at muddying the waters for posterity, so the truth is almost impossible to prise out of its shell. Ostensibly, during the row, Frank became physically violent; it wouldn't have been the first time.

Right: Sinatra Gets ready for a performance of the Frank Sinatra Show

"Columnist says Sinatra boots Ava out of home."

Sinatra was then said to be throwing up in the bathroom. Two spoiled children left home alone without their parents for the night.

Frank was misery personified.

On October the 27th there was a rally for Adlai Stevenson, at that point in the middle of an election campaign. And there were Frank and Ava, too: *"I can introduce a wonderful, wonderful man. I'm a great fan of his myself. Ladies and gentlemen, my husband, Frank Sinatra!"*

When it was over, Frank was still misery personified... and unemployed. He was shredding his nerves waiting to hear from Harry Cohn, knowing that other actors were being tested for the role. He was depressed. Ava was about to go to Africa for filming; he could feel that she was already moving away from him emotionally, too.

When Ava went to Africa, one of almost 600 cast and crew, Frank went with her, anxious, riddled with inferiority, frightened of what might happen between Ava and Clark Gable. On that account, he need have had no worries whatsoever.

Life was no fun for him one way or the other, and he spent his time in Africa whilst Ava was shooting the movie, sitting in a chair worrying about From Here to Eternity, irritated by insects and dirt, and arguing with Ava over drinks at night until she swore at him and told him to just get on with his life.

And then the telegram came.

He was getting a screen test for the coveted role of Maggio.

He had to ask Ava to give him money for the plane ticket home. On Friday, November the 14th, Frank left Africa. The gods had finally taken pity on their plaything.

Left: Sinatra and wife Ava Gardner, leaving London for a trip to Africa, where Ava is to make the film Mogambo with Clarke Gable

Opposite page: Sinatra in publicity portrait as Maggio for the film 'From Here To Eternity', 1953

Those Whom the Gods Love Grow Young

Oscar Wilde.

What Frank didn't know, was that Ava was pregnant.

There was no question of her remaining in that condition for long. She was also a plaything of the gods, if not almost one of them; she knew she wanted it to stay that way. She was having the time of her life, relishing a role that was tailor-made for her, and she knew she was good in it. *"... This is not the time, and I'm not ready"* she said to her director John Ford when he tried to talk her out of an abortion.

She never would be.

Frank took his screen test. It was, apparently nothing more than all right. But the director, Fred Zimmerman, thought otherwise. Everyone had been bowled over by Eli Wallach's screen test. But when the producer, Buddy Adler, watched Frank do the test again, he, too, was convinced. Harry Cohn was out of town; the waiting game began.

In London, Ava recovered from her abortion. Frank still did not know. She didn't tell him when he rang.

Before he returned to Africa, Frank visited Nancy, brought presents for the children and did some concerts. He was still popular with the ladies... And still unable to resist their beds. He missed Ava. He never found a contradiction between those two aspects of his life. Or he simply ignored it. Ava was missing Frank less and less, and found less and less reason to remain either bored or faithful. She was

30 years old and at the top of the tree.

It was Christmas 1952 and Frank returned to Africa to try and remain calm whilst he waited for the word on his screen test. For once the gossip columnists had something good to say about him. *"... I think he's just right for the part"* was Hedda Hopper's opinion. He whiled away his time in Africa by organising a Christmas show and singing Christmas carols.

Ava discovered she was pregnant again.

One thing she knew; it certainly wasn't because of Frank. He was apparently delighted. He sang to her before he left for the States, she said.

Years later, with sad self recognition, Ava would say, *"MGM had all sorts of penalty clauses about their stars having babies... We couldn't even take care of ourselves. How were we going to take care of a baby?"*

That pregnancy would end as the first one had.

Frank's nail biting continued back in America; two singing gigs in Boston and Montréal, all he had been able to drum up, distracted his burning thoughts a little.

Bert Allen from the William Morris Agency called; the dice had fallen.

Frank Sinatra had landed the greatest movie role of his life.

Ava was in London getting ready for a second hospital visit when Frank caught up with her. He found out about the pregnancy, of course, but there was no way he could stop her from the planned course of action. Sinatra's daughter Nancy wrote that Ava had said, *"I'll never forget waking up after the operation and seeing Frank sitting next to the bed with tears in his eyes"*. Tears of pain, no doubt, tears of hurt pride, tears of anger.

Afterwards they shared an uneasy peace in Paris. Then he was gone.

April 1953 was indeed the turning point for Sinatra. He signed a 7-year contract with Capitol Records giving him a 5% royalty and he began a new era in his singing career with his voice now mature and full. One of the many songs that he recorded was **Three Coins in the Fountain**. It would become an Academy Award winner, a huge success.

For the first time in his life, perhaps, Sinatra behaved himself on the set of a film. He took his own advice well, because his career depended on it and he knew it. One of his co-stars in the film was the brilliant Montgomery Clift, and he and Sinatra were soon close pals, *"... A mutual admiration thing"* as Frank described it, two exquisite and professionally sensitive artists working together. Frank understood that he needed this extraordinary actor's help to pull off his coup, and Clift selflessly and tirelessly rehearsed Sinatra's dialogue with him like a piece of music, taking him through the rhythms, the dynamics, the pauses, the ebb and flow of every second. It wasn't Frank's style of rehearsal, but he had the intelligence to know what he was being given. This amazing opportunity to give life to a dramatic role could be his lifesaver; literally. Also, he was frightened, there was everything to play for, everything to lose.

The two men, steel willed in avoiding alcohol during working hours, also sealed their friendship over drinks off the set. Together with the author of the book, James Jones, the trio could hardly be prised apart; the alcohol brought them even closer together. Their

friendship, and being put to bed dead drunk by Jones, a habit that continued throughout the shooting by all accounts, seemed to be enough for Frank, because he didn't succumb to the temptation that usually prevented him from exercising 'good husbandry'. He kept his good behaviour record intact during the filming and was even sweet to the journalists. The only times he reverted to his old ways were, firstly, when he suddenly announced that he was buying into the Sands in Las Vegas an interesting move this because with no money and the IRS tax authorities claiming back tax, where would those dollars come from, some 54,000 of them? Perhaps he did have *"friends"* in low places. Why did they pop up now and not when he was down and out?

The second relapse came when he was forced by the director, Fred Zinnemann, and Cohn, to perform a crucial scene in the film sitting down, so that the impact would be reduced; Cohn had insisted, and the whole film was at stake. Sinatra blew a fuse but had to fall in line. Sinatra didn't understand then, but Fred Zinnemann had saved Frank and the film and, therefore, probably Frank's career, by getting

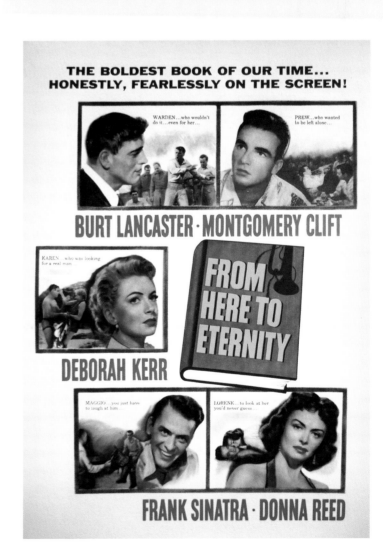

Top Left: Fred_Zinnemann

Right: Original movie poster for From Here to Eternity

the singer to bend in the wind just a little.

The wind, as it turned out, was now blowing in Frank's direction again, although many people worked in the background to make it happen. One of those was Alan Livingston of MCA. He brought the musical genius that was Nelson Riddle into Sinatra's orbit, though he had to override the singer's prejudice and sneak Riddle in under the radar to do it. Frank should have been eternally grateful he did so. When Sinatra went into the recording studio, it took one song, "I've got the World on a String", and Frank was mesmerised by Riddle's arrangements. This was new, this was exciting and Frank felt it. *"I'm back! I'm back, baby, I'm back"*, he is said to have enthused. Not quite, but he soon would be.

Ominously, his neuroses, too, shook themselves and settled in for another round.

What of Ava in all this excitement?

Ava had discovered Europe, and its gentler, less neurotic style of living suited her. She wouldn't go back to the States anymore to live. She had a flat in Regent's Park in London. She and Frank met in the English capital, where they were going to embark on a *"second honeymoon"*, during a break in filming for Knights of the Round Table. The road to hell… as the saying goes.

They went off to Rome for Frank to do a round of concerts. It started off well. Frank punched a photographer in the face. Half-full venues greeted him; it wasn't him, it was Ava they wanted to see. Marital jealousy flared. The booing started in Italy… Frank walked off the stage and had to be persuaded to return. More booing in Sweden; the show in Denmark tanked, he was broke. Ava was earning almost $20,000 a week in her film. In an atmosphere of mutual disappointment and dislike, they returned to London. Frank zipped around the country from gig to gig. Britain appreciated him, at least. Their welcome did him good. His relationship with Ava didn't, and the inevitable arguments led to a final bust up in London. Frank left for America, where From Here to Eternity had just premiered.

He returned to a hero's reception.

The film reviews glowed. Suddenly, work was being thrown in his direction; films, TV, radio, concerts. He was back alright. The old Frank was back. As Ava said, *"Now that he's successful again, he's become his old arrogant self"*. They joined up again in the USA; they were together and tormenting each other. Sinatra's rage wasn't focused just on Ava,

Left: Ernest Borgnine, confronts Burt Lancaster with a knife, while Frank watches on in a scene from Fred Zinnemann's From Here to Eternity

Above & Right: Sinatra poses for a portrait

though. When he lost a role in On the Waterfront, Sam Spiegel came in for Sinatra's wrath, and with no one to hit, according to his valet, he wrecked his own living room.

The only constant in his inconstant life was the family he had abandoned, and he phoned his children every day. Even for them he was the Voice.

For Ava, too, he had become a voice on a telephone, screaming, agonizing, crying. He provoked her once too often with his conquest one night. Ava hung up.

On October the 27th 1953, it was MGM who announced, *"Their separation is final and Miss Gardner will seek a divorce".*

So came the quiet death of a turbulent love.

Sinatra's new career was already under way, although he could not know that he was already in the town that would raise him up to the heights again; Las Vegas. He was appearing at the Sands, partly owned by the *"... hoodlum responsible for giving me a job"*, as he put it, Sam Giancana. Sinatra brought a buzz to the place and that was the buzz of money for the owners. The Sands and its coffers filled when Frank sang. The owners were doubtless extremely happy to have him as an equity partner. And he acted in a way his partners could sympathise with when he found out that Ava had had a drink with Peter Lawford. He picked up the phone and screamed at Lawford that he was going to send someone over to break his legs. He was still obsessed with Ava and he was often living on pills, cigarettes, booze and coffee, frantic to regain his lost place in paradise with his goddess. Whilst he recorded a twice-weekly radio show, Perfectly Frank, he feigned good humour, lived through emotional hell.

Ava, however, longing to get out of America and put her marriage behind her, was ecstatic, because she had landed the film role she had craved; as Maria Vargas opposite Humphrey Bogart as Harry Dawes in The Barefoot Contessa, to shoot in Europe. Sinatra went into a slump when he found out. Manie Sacks had once found Sinatra crying on the kitchen floor. When Jimmy Van Heusen went to see him, he found him on the kitchen floor, too; his arm soaked in blood.

Sinatra had slit his wrist.

Money moved around swiftly to keep the lid on this episode, too, and Frank Sinatra was taken to Mount Sinai Hospital in Washington suffering from *"exhaustion"*. A half-truth, but no lie. His weight had dropped to 118 pounds. Ava agreed to meet him at her sister Bappie's place. In her head, Ava was no longer even in the country let alone still with Sinatra. Soon, she was gone from him and America and so was her wedding ring.

All he could do was sing, and in exquisite voice he sang himself a major hit in December when he recorded Young at Heart to a superb Nelson Riddle arrangement. A new relationship was born.

But as far as Frank was concerned the old one wasn't yet dead. He chased Ava to Madrid where she was spending Christmas with her new beau, Luis Dominguin. Frank lied to himself and the reporters. Ava didn't want to see him, was furious to be interrupted. They returned to Rome to talk, shout and maybe try reconciliation. But as the new year of 1954 tentatively raised its own voice, Sinatra quietly slipped back to America, and his album Songs for Young Lovers was released.

He knew he had lost Ava.

His career was beginning to fire on all cylinders; Young at Heart was on the Billboard chart and rising, and the offers coming in included roles in Guys and Dolls and Pal Joey. The number of concerts increased, and Riddle's creative genius inspired the singer to even greater vocal peaks. Sinatra filled in the time until the Oscar awards in March visiting boxing matches, racetracks and... he paid for sexual pleasures.

Then the 25th arrived and brought the glitterati to Hollywood and probably the most important and overwhelming moment in Sinatra's life. When the winners were announced he felt the earth move.

The winner for best supporting actor was Frank Sinatra.

That night, at the height of his success to date, he wandered off alone with his trophy along the streets of Beverley Hills. Alone in his glittering cage, and lonely without the only woman he loved.

Alone was a scary word for Sinatra, and he exerted almost as much effort on avoiding being in that state as he did on his career. Ava had bewitched him; he never wanted to let that happen again. Soon, the heiress Gloria Vanderbildt had swum into view, and falling under his charm spell she was soon arriving at glitterati events on his arm. It lasted just a few weeks. A string of other women followed her, courted with gifts and tantalised by the high life; Marlene Dietrich and Zsa Zsa Gabor amongst them. If the girls were just starting out in the movies, he would exchange sex for work. Years later, actress Eva Bartok would maintain that her daughter Deana was Sinatra's child. He never acknowledged or denied it.

There was, of course, one other great affair in these interim years between marriage number two to Ava and number three to Mia Farrow in 1966; Lauren Bacall.

Right: Sinatra and Donna Reed pose for a portrait after winning best supporting actor and best supporting actress Oscars, for their roles in 'From Here To Eternity', March 25, 1954 in Hollywood

Money Can't Buy You Love

During the period when he staggered around in the devastated emotional landscape that Ava had left behind, Frank almost moved in with the Bogarts, whom he had known since the end of WWII, by which time the couple had been married for nine years. The educated Bogart fascinated Sinatra, who was extremely aware of his own lack of education. Sinatra's self-indulgence was soon too much for even Bogart to endure and they almost came to blows. Nonetheless, Sinatra became part of a hand-picked coterie that had formed around Bogart, and from the laughter and drinking developed the group that came to be dubbed 'The Holmby Hills Rat Pack', dedicated to being *"… Against everything and everyone, including themselves"*. The original group included Judy Garland, and Sinatra became the Pack Master and Bacall the Den Mother. *"Never Rat on a Rat"* was the motto on their specially designed crest.

For Sinatra, there began the third phase of his tempestuous career. Even though his emotional life would enter no calmer waters, by 1954, his film career was on an upward spiral when he appeared in a movie with Doris Day named after his hit song of the previous year, Young at Heart, followed by Suddenly, and a film that would bring him more accolades, The Man with the Golden Arm. He played the lead character, Frankie Machine, and garnered an Academy Award nomination as Best Actor in a Leading Role and a BAFTA nomination for Best Actor. And he took another role that was right up his street; that of Nathan Detroit in the hit film musical Guys and Dolls with Marlon Brando and Jean Simmons. The film was ranked as the number 1 moneymaking film of 1956 by Variety.

Frank's regard for Sammy Davis Jr. was evident again in 1954 when Davis was involved in a car crash that almost killed him, and did cause him to lose his left eye. After Frank had visited him in hospital, Davis, who *"had no place to go"*, in his own words, was taken to Sinatra's home in Palm Springs to recover, and Sinatra found Davis his own place to live and encouraged him to continue performing. For Davis, Sinatra was untouchable... but he was not unaware of Frank's ugly side, and he did not approve of it.

The singing of a confident Sinatra was to be heard in all its finery on two albums recorded in 1954, Songs for Young Lovers and Swing Easy! Both albums went to number 3 on the American charts, with Billboard, Metronome and Down Beat voting him top male vocalist.

His vocal mastery was then focused on his first 12-inch LP, In the Wee Small Hours, acknowledged as one of the first concept albums

Above: Original theatrical release poster for the 1959 movie, The Man with the Golden Arm, by Saul Bass

Opposite page: promotional portrait for director Lewis Allen's film, 'Suddenly'. Sinatra plays a hit man in the film.

Above & left: As Frankie Machine in 'The Man With The Golden Arm', directed by Otto Preminger, 1955

that he began to record in Hollywood in February 1955; it dealt with such themes as night life, loneliness, love lost, introspection and failed relationships, all part of the more sombre song panorama that Sinatra had been keen to record to help expand his repertoire and establish himself on a different level from the one his bobby-soxer persona had inhabited. Wisely; for after all, rock 'n roll had thundered onto the music scene and Elvis Presley was the new king king of a music genre, incidentally, that a bewildered Sinatra reportedly *"… hated so much"*; *"phoney"*, *"false"*, *"dirty"*, *"degenerate"*, were just some of the adjectives he used for the new music trend sweeping America.

Sinatra's album rose to number 2 on the US charts and remained

there for eighteen weeks, also scoring a tremendous commercial success for the singer. His income rocketed. A TV deal brought him $7 million over three years and the movies brought in more. Now Bing Crosby could be heard saying that Sinatra might be the greatest entertainer of all time. Oh, how sweet the sound.

Early in 1956, wanting to manage his own movie career, Sinatra formed Kent Productions.

What mixed sentiments Sinatra must have experienced when Humphrey Bogart was told in February 1956 that he had throat cancer and less than one year to live, no one truly knows. Sinatra visited Bogart often, keeping his spirits up by regaling him with the exploits of the other Rat Pack members. Bogart was jealous of Sinatra; with good reason, as it turned out. As Bogart deteriorated, Sinatra was going from strength to strength, and the Rat Pack, with a different cast, would soon be associated only with his name.

This was another year to remember for the singer turned actor; he was awarded the Golden Globe for Best Actor in a Motion Picture Musical or Comedy for his role as Joey Evans in Pal Joey. By the end of the year he had recorded 63 more songs.

Another name had entered into Sinatra's orbit and joined in the fun by 1957. Frank appeared in Los Angeles alongside another smooth Italian crooner, who had enjoyed enormous success as part of a duo with comic Jerry Lewis, from whom he had parted company in 1956; his name was Dean Martin. Martin, together with Sammy Davis Jr., Shirley MacLaine, Joey Bishop and Peter Lawford would become the new Rat Pack led by Sinatra. It was the same Peter Lawford who had met Ava Gardner as a friend only to have an irate Frank on the phone threatening *"… I'll have your legs broken, you bum"*, a threat that three years later had squeezed almost the only apology from Sinatra that anyone could remember. That abrupt about-turn of an apology, by the way, now seems self-serving in retrospect; Lawford was Senator John F. Kennedy's brother-in-law, a man in whom Frank was very interested, and for whom, it was obvious, there were great things in store.

Was it Martin's background that attracted Sinatra to him? Having engaged in prizefighting, running bootleg Mafia whiskey, gambling, he dealt blackjack and worked a craps table with the warning, *"Your son's gonna be a gangster"*, ringing in his ears. Dean was someone that Sinatra could relate to. But although the two men spent a great deal of time together later, Martin had his life, and himself, under control. He admired Sinatra greatly as a singer, said Dean's second wife, but *"… didn't respect him as a man"*. Time Magazine, closing in on Frank's psyche, had perspicaciously written, *"There's nothing inside (Sinatra). He puts out so terrifically that nothing can accumulate inside"*. Cannot; or was not allowed to?

Humphrey Bogart died on the 14th of January 1957; Sinatra didn't

attend the funeral; perhaps his conscience was playing games with him, because by then he and Bacall had been having an affair for some time. *"We just hoped Bogie wouldn't find out"*, said Bacall years later. Bogart had suspected it, nonetheless, and although *"Frank loved Bogart"*, as one of Frank's ex-girlfriends said, as far as women or his career were concerned, Frank would go over dead bodies. In this case, he practically did.

By the spring of 1957, Bacall and he were dating. Yet his behaviour was as erratic as ever; on off arrangements, flowers, fights with whoever displeased him for whatever reason, attentive and then distant.

Battling his demons, longing still for the stability that he craved from others but was unable to provide, fourteen months after her husband's death, Frank proposed to Lauren on March 11th 1958. And then she made a fatal mistake by admitting the proposal to a

Above: Lauren Bacall and Humphrey Bogart in a scene from 'Dark Passage'

Opposite page: Dean Martin

Right: Lauren Bacall

newspaperman; it hit the headlines next day. Sinatra fumed, called her to regale her with accusations, and from then on, refused to speak to Bacall for six years. She had instantly become *"... that pushy female."* *"Frank"*, said Bacall, who had now joined the ranks of those who knew him better than the fans, *"was juvenile and insecure"*. Bogart had been *"... a grown up"* man. Funny thing, love.

Shirley MacLaine, with whom Frank made the movie Some Came Running in 1958, remembered Sinatra's boorish, cruel and juvenile behaviour during the months of shooting, none of which was ever directed at her or the bellboys, who could invariably rely on a $100 tip, as the Rat Pack, originally dubbed 'The Clan', cemented its reputation. The girls were on tap for Frank, those in the audiences often throwing their keys onto the stage; but significantly, the majority of those who found their way to his side were professionals; no emotional involvement required.

Emotion had been unavoidable when Manie Sacks died in February of that year after a fight against leukemia. Sinatra didn't shun the contact with near death, closing down the production of the film he was making and flying down to see the dying man who had been such a vital part of his life for so long; one of the men who had helped to steer him and his career.

Sinatra went back into the studio for his next album, Frank Sinatra Sings for Only the Lonely, which was released in September. It soared into the Billboard album chart and went to number 1. In total it was in the charts for 120 weeks, and included such classics as "One for My Baby (And One More for the Road)", and "Angel Eyes". Frank's Midas touch had returned with a vengeance. (The album was certified Gold four years later.)

Frank now stated publicly that Senator Kennedy was *"... a friend of mine"*. *"Jack's pimp"*, was how Peter Lawford put it, introducing Kennedy to glamorous women and discreet prostitutes and later helping to smooth the way to Mafia contacts such as Joe Fischetti. Another of Sinatra's impenetrable relationships was forming.

Sinatra's career was now rolling high and Las Vegas was to become the new stomping ground for his talent. The coming decade would prove to be one of soaring highlights, success and laughter. Dean Martin and Frank appeared together at The Sands in Las Vegas for the first time in January 1959, and he starred opposite Steve McQueen in "Never so Few" in July. The highlights that year came thick and fast, after he had recorded another song that was to become a lasting favourite, "High Hopes"; it stayed in the hot 100 list for 17 weeks and gained him an Academy Award for Best Original Song. Also, three Grammy awards came his way for Album of the

Right: Members of the 'Rat Pack' perform on stage at The Sands, Las Vegas, L-R: Sammy Davis Jr., Joey Bishop, Frank Sinatra, Peter Lawford and Dean Martin

Above: Frank 1960

Opposite page: Frank 1958

Above: A poster for Lewis Milestone's 1960 crime film 'Ocean's 11' starring Frank Sinatra, Dean Martin, Sammy Davis Jr., Peter Lawford, and Angie Dickinson

Opposite page: Promotional portrait of the cast of the film, 'Oceans 11'

Year, Best Male Vocal Performance, and a Special Award: Artists and Repertoire Contribution for "Come Dance with Me".

In Frank's eyes, his personal status also rose enormously that year, when in November, John Kennedy was a guest at his house in Palm Springs after a fundraising bout in Los Angeles; a visit that evidently filled Sinatra with pride, as a plaque was placed on Kennedy's bedroom door that stated, *"John F. Kennedy Slept Here"*. Sinatra's contribution to Kennedy's election campaign would prove to be greater than that of any entertainer in any presidential campaign.

In January of the New Year 1960, a legendary show premiered at the Sands Hotel in Las Vegas. "Summit at the Sands" starred Joey Bishop, Sammy Davis Jr., Peter Lawford, Dean Martin and Frank Sinatra, through whose hands a host of top-ranking guest stars passed. The five members of the Rat Pack were starring in the film Ocean's 11 that was being shot that year, partly in the Sands Hotel. When Kennedy dropped in to see a show, the carousing with Sinatra and the boys continued into the night, causing Kennedy's campaign team the largest of headaches in the attempt to keep their candidate's 'activities' out of the press.

What also needed to be kept out of the press was the contact between John Kennedy's father Joe and Frank Sinatra. Kennedy senior had asked Sinatra to help his boy win the election. In his words *"… A boost from our friends in Chicago who control the unions. They can win this race for us."* Sinatra agreed to help out, and during a golf game with Sam Giancana he sealed the deal. Money began to flow like water to the democratic wallet, and according to those in contact with Sinatra at the time, a lot of it passed through the singer's hands. He seemed to enjoy the cut and thrust of political wrangling, the wheeling and dealing, and excelled at fundraising, often offering a performance by himself as the reward for donors putting down the dollars. His energy was boundless, and even when he was filming the insipid movie, The Devil at 4 O'Clock, he would jump into his private plane during his free hours and continue the campaigning on Hawaii. Frank remembered this period as *"… the most exciting assignment of my life"*.

His career certainly wasn't on hold, however, and between March and April he was back in the studio in Hollywood to record Nice 'n' Easy, an LP containing, almost exclusively, ballads arranged and conducted by Nelson Riddle. It stayed at number 1 on the Billboard stereo album chart for 9 weeks and was nominated for a Grammy Award as Album of the Year, Best Male Vocal Performance, Best Arrangement.

But Sinatra was growing discontented at Capital Records, wanting more artistic freedom, and he decided to break out. He formed his own record label Reprise Records, with which he intended to record his own and his Rat Pack friends' songs. The first album for the new company, Ring-A-Ding-Ding!, was recorded in March and consisted of upbeat swing numbers with evergreens such as "In the Still of the Night", "A Fine Romance" and "A Foggy Day (in London Town)". It was released in December and reached number 4 in the charts.

Nancy Jr. married in September to singer Tommy Sands, and Sinatra, at last, was there for his daughter, to give her away.

In November, there was more great excitement for Frank, firstly because Kennedy beat Richard Nixon to the presidency by 113,057 votes. And to quote one Chicago mobster, *"… more than a few arms and legs were broken"* to get those votes. And Frank's role? Sinatra apparently felt that he had enough influence with Kennedy to assure Giancana that the new administration would back away from an FBI investigation into the mobster's activities. He was wrong. Robert Kennedy, the man Frank had called a *"little weasel"*, became attorney general, and the pursuit of Giancana continued more intensely than before. The Mafia man was more than a little upset, and considered that Frank Sinatra was, in part at least, responsible for his having his been hoodwinked.

The second event was the marriage of Sammy Davis Jr., a man who Sinatra had chaperoned through his career to such an extent that Davis practically became a member of the Sinatra family. Frank was Davis's best man at the wedding on the 13th November.

In January 1961, Kennedy was inaugurated. Even though Sinatra had persuaded a host of stars to attend a pre-inauguration gala that would take $1.7 million off the Democratic Party debt, he was not invited to the ceremony itself. Frank had reluctantly also asked Sammy Davis Jr. to postpone his marriage to the white Swedish actress May Britt until after the election, under pressure from the Kennedy camp. Davis did so. It was then made clear to Davis that his presence at the inauguration was not desired, either. Frank was embittered by this betrayal. One of Sinatra's most endearing characteristics was his support for African Americans both publicly and privately in the struggle for equal rights. He often made speeches about desegregation, and Rat Pack members would boycott hotels and casinos that barred black performers and patrons. Sinatra, it seemed, had been used by the Kennedys, and early 1961, he reaped his reward when, so the story goes, he was sent the skinned head of a lamb by some unhappy Kennedy sponsors. Unsurprisingly, the relationship between Kennedy and Sinatra had begun to come apart at the seams. A break that was compounded when Kennedy cancelled plans to stay with Frank in 1962 and holed up at Bing Crosby's ranch instead. Sinatra, we are told, went into a

Right: Frank Relaxing in Hollywood, California, 1963

crazed rage like a *"maniacal king"*.

Meanwhile, there was Juliet Prowse, an Anglo-Indian actress and dancer, to occupy his emotional life and soothe those rages. They had met on the set of Can-Can in 1959 and even announced their engagement that year of 1962. It was a short one. Prowse, ostensibly, wanted to concentrate on her career; she was more flattered than in love, she said afterwards, adding that her famous beau could be *"very difficult"* after a few drinks.

So, alone in a crowd again.

That didn't stop him from going on a ten-country fund-raising trip, the World Tour for Children, which brought in almost $6 million, displaying the other side, the more humane side, of his fractured personality. Doubtless the padrone in him was humoured, too, by the pleasure of giving.

As far as the Kennedys were concerned, it came to the point that no matter how Sinatra twisted and turned to try and influence them, his efforts fell on deaf ears, and ominously, Giancana no longer believed a word he said. A dangerous situation. Being ordered to appear at a mob-run venue was a generous punishment in the circumstances. Fortunately, Bobby Kennedy, unsure of the damage he might unleash, never turned the full heat of his legal gaze on Sinatra.

Christmas that year showed where Sinatra's interests lay when he spent the holiday period in Acapulco with a group of wealthy and influential people, one of whom was Sam Giancana who was bringing Sinatra a lot of trouble.

Frank owned a share of the Cal-Neva Lodge and Casino on Lake Tahoe on the Nevada-California border; that is, Frank's share was probably a Giancana/Frank-owned share. When Frank lost his temper with Ed Olsen, chairman of the Gaming Control Board, he brought their wrath down on his head. Giancana was banned from all Nevada casinos, and Sinatra had dug himself into a hole; he was forced to unload his financial interests in Cal-Neva and stripped of his licenses. The financial hit was severe, but it didn't stop Sinatra from associating with Giancana, flying him around in his private plane or from hosting him in Palm Springs.

Despite all this turbulence and worry in his life, Sinatra's career continued unabated its intensity. Between the years of 1961 and the end of 1964, he completed 9 films, including "The Manchurian Candidate", which he considered to be the *"... finest picture I have ever made"*, and "Come Blow Your Horn", which brought him a nomination for a Golden Globe Award for Best Actor Motion Picture Musical or Comedy. The Rat Pack performances continued at The Sands Hotel and he joined forces with jazz piano

Above: Poster for the 1962 movie, 'The Manchurian Candidate'

Right: Frank Sinatra drags a soaking wet Laurence Harvey from the lake during filming of John Frankenheimer thriller 'The Manchurian Candidate' in Central Park

legend Count Basie for the Sinatra Basie album, which proved to be so popular and successful that they repeated the trick in 1964 with It Might As Well Be Swing. He also appeared on television and visited eleven other countries for singing engagements whilst nurturing his Reprise Records company along as well. Reprise proved to a very worthwhile enterprise. Ten albums in three years were produced by Sinatra, and he sold the company to Warner Brothers Records in August 1963, making himself $6 million dollars. He may have had no choice, as he owed Warner Brothers money, but it also had the consequence of earning him the highest pay packet of any Hollywood actor-entertainer.

It was while he was filming Robin and the 7 Hoods, playing a mobster of all things, that Sinatra heard the news that Kennedy had been assassinated. He wandered off alone before finishing his day's work and then going home to Palm Springs, where he stayed for several days with bottles of Jack Daniels to console him, thinking no doubt, of what might have been, of the fun and laughter, the waste of life, of the betrayal.

But the gods of fame had not finished toying with him and had far worse things to torment him with.

On Sunday night, the 8th December 1963, Sinatra's son Frank Jr. was kidnapped at gunpoint from a lodge at Lake Tahoe. What his father went through in the following seven days in torment and fear for his son's life can only be imagined, as he took calls from the kidnappers and dealt with the demands for ransom money. Frank was agonised by the thought that the mob were sending him a message. Giancana had never forgiven Frank for the fallout from the Kennedy election, and Frank only had Giancana's east coast pals to thank for the fact that he did not end up as another mafia murder statistic. He was, as Giancana put it, *"... lucky to be alive"*. If the mob were behind the kidnap, what would they do to his son? Giancana had offered to help find Frank Jr. A cynical move? Frank senior had the FBI take over.

$240,000 changed hands, and Frank Jr. was deposited outside his mother's house in Bel Air. Amateurs at work, as it turned out, who were caught and imprisoned.

For a reprise, the gods then decided to play with the great man personally. Whilst holidaying on Hawaii, he went to help a woman in difficulties in the surf and then he almost drowned, too. He was dragged out more dead than alive, his lungs full of water, and suffering from hypoxia lack of oxygen in the brain.

Which seemed to be the same state he had been in before he even entered the water.

Money Can't Buy You Love

Left: Sinatra and musician Count Basie backstage

A Love of His Own Briefly

Frank Sinatra in the mid sixties was a giant in American show business, an untouchable star, physically no journalist dare to denigrate him or there might be threatening phone calls and professionally, who could demand and get the terms he stated for film roles and singing contracts. He presided over a plethora of companies from Reprise Records to film production companies and was estimated to be earning $3.5 million per year in 1965, the year of his fiftieth birthday.

It was a good year. It was the year he starred in Von Ryan's Express and made his directorial debut, the only film he ever directed, None but the Brave. In June he was in St Louis for a concert with Dean Martin and Sammy Davis Jr. to raise funds for Dismas House, which was a prisoner rehabilitation and training centre, particularly for African-Americans. He recorded the album September of My Years, which won the Grammy award for Album of the Year. It Was a Very Good Year was the single from the album that won the Grammy Award for Best Vocal Performance, Male, in 1966.

1965 was a very good year for his love life, too, because his next attempt at marital stability was not far off. Whilst filming Von Ryan's Express in Los Angeles in October, he was re-acquainted with a young 19-year-old actress; Mia Farrow. According to Farrow, Frank asked her to fly to Palm Springs with him that very same evening, and within a short space of time they were spending their weekends together over crossword puzzles and Vaughan Williams symphonies.

Frank's birthday was in December. He was 50, his smooth baritone voice now *"like torn velvet"* according to the writer Arnold Shore,

and Frank himself was expressing thoughts such as *"... Frankly, I'm getting a bit tired"*. Ava, the only woman he had loved, by his own admission was turning into an alcoholic. He was aware, too, that just as rock 'n' roll had done in the 50s, the new arrivals, the Beatles, were churning up the music scene in the 60s; Frank Sinatra was a has-been for the new young music listeners of the era. What might the future hold for this heavyweight icon of popular music? At his birthday party he drank very heavily. His new girlfriend was not there to pick him up when he fell over that night. What role in his complicated psyche had she been allotted?

Perhaps *"Angel Face"*, as he called Mia Farrow, brought with her a refreshing sense of youth and innocence that poured balm into his problematic existence. Maybe, but the constant drinking, his circle of friends, who were mostly 40 years her senior, the incessant gambling and socialising was wearing for Mia, as were the references to their age difference Dean Martin quipped that he had a bottle of Scotch that was older than Mia.

Inevitably, Frank had an affair, and prostitutes; she went on a trip with someone younger. Almost as inevitably, they found their way back together and, of course, he asked her to marry him. She accepted the proposal and an $85,000 diamond engagement ring. Everyone, it seemed, including Frank, saw the writing on the wall before they were even married. He asked Shirley MacLaine to meet his fiancée and give her opinion of Farrow. Hardly the actions of a man head over heels in love. In love was what he was with Ava Gardner, still, and with whom he was meeting up, even at this

stage, and by whom he was still being put through the mangle. Sinatra's friend Brad Dexter told Frank he should see a psychiatrist rather than get married, a comment which, predictably, had Sinatra in a rage, and by the next morning he was on his way to get married. On the 19th of July 1966, a four-minute ceremony at the Sands Hotel made Frank and Mia man and wife.

Exactly how bad a mistake it was for them to marry was soon made clear to a Las Vegas audience; *"I finally found a broad I could cheat on".* It was probably one of the most distasteful sentences Sinatra uttered in public and absolutely humiliating for Mia. There were rumours; physical abuse against Mia. She denied them. For their own reasons they had trapped one another; but she was becoming a flower power rock 'n' roll chick and he was swerving to the political right. Both suffered the lonely consequences and an estrangement that was dragged out for two years. The marriage finally breathed its last breath when Mia refused to finish work prematurely on her film Rosemary's Baby, to go and work on a movie that Frank was making. Sinatra's lawyer turned up on the set of Rosemary's Baby with the divorce papers, which Mia signed immediately. Frank wanted to be married, he had admitted to friends. Yet he was unwilling, perhaps incapable, of investing of himself in the commitment required to fill the reservoir of support and friendship that everyone needs.

Mia, it seemed, didn't suffer long, for she was soon in India with the Maharishi and the Beatles.

Sinatra's suffering had settled in for the long haul. People noticed how lonely he seemed to be in the bubble of his power and fame. The world, it seemed, could be wooed by him but not bent to his will. He was emotionally incoherent.

In contrast, his career was in full flood. There were films to be made and there were three Grammy Awards: Album of the Year for "September of My Years", Best Male Vocal Performance for "It Was A Very Good Year", and the Grammy Lifetime Achievement Award. Also, the single release of "Strangers in the Night" went to number 1 and stayed there for fifteen weeks, and "That's Life" hit number 4 in the singles charts. In 1967 there was a chart-topping duet with his daughter Nancy, Somethin' Stupid, and in 1968, My Way surged upwards to find new ears to be persuaded to listen to his voice. Sinatra said that he disliked My Way, he didn't like to boast. Was he being disingenuous, or was he really the only person who couldn't see a connection between him and the song? Perhaps it was simply too painfully close to the bone for him to admit as much. He was never a good judge of his own character, the lot of all those whose egos inflate and fly away with them.

Left: The Beatles

Right: Mia Farrow

Next page: Frank and Mia on deck of the yacht, Southern Breeze, 1965

Above: Frank getting kissed by Dean Martin 1965

Left: Directing musicians of the Count Basie Orchestra at a rehearsal with arranger-conductor Quincy Jones, at a sound stage in Los Angeles, California, 1965

Next Page: Frank Sinatra, Trevor Howard and others in a scene from the film 'Von Ryan's Express', 1965

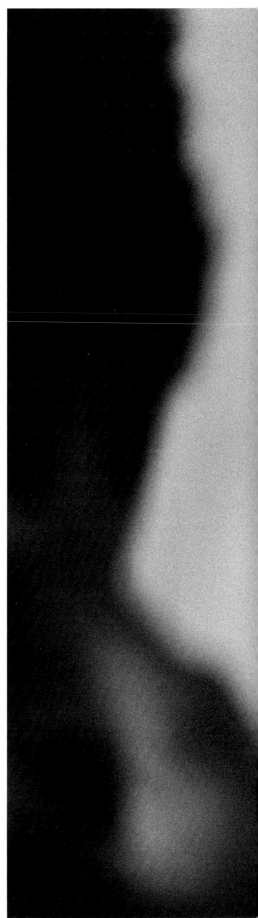

Above: On set of his film 'Marriage on the Rocks', directed by
Jack Donohue, Burbank, California, 1965

Left: St. Louis, Missouri for a Frank Sinatra Benefit Concert, 1965

Left: Performing live onstage at the Newport Jazz Festival, 1965

Above: With Dean Martin during recording of 'The Dean Martin Variety Show' 1967

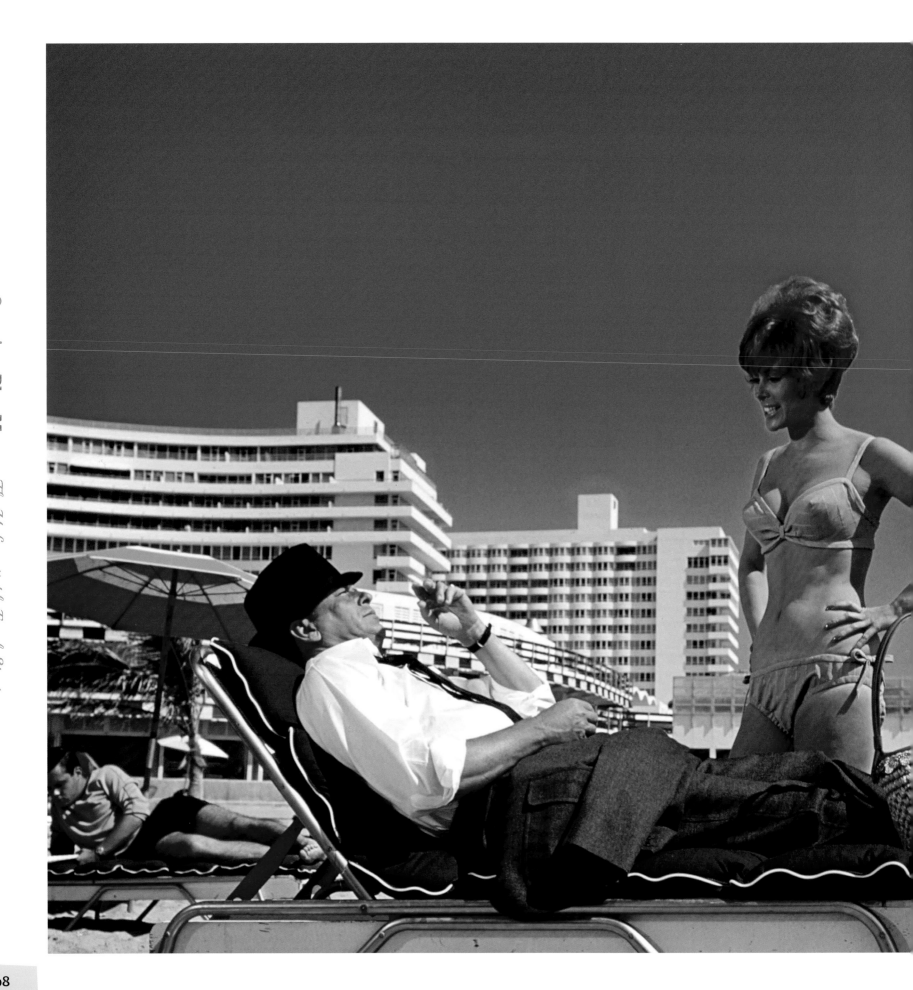

SINATRA:THE NAKED RUNNER

Slowly they stripped Sam Laker down until there was nothing but animal left...

Featuring PETER VAUGHAN · DERREN NESBITT · NADIA GRAY · TOBY ROBINS · INGER STRATTON · Based on the novel by FRANCIS CLIFFORD
Screenplay by STANLEY MANN · Produced by BRAD DEXTER · Directed by SIDNEY J. FURIE · A SINATRA ENTERPRISES PRODUCTION WB
TECHNICOLOR® TECHNISCOPE® From WARNER BROS.

Property of National Screen Service Corp. Licensed for display only in connection with
the exhibition of this picture at your theatre. Must be returned immediately thereafter.   67/225

A Love of His Own. Briefly

Above: poster for Sidney J. Furie's 1967 drama 'The Naked Runner' starring Frank Sinatra

Left: Sinatra as 'Tony Rome' laying on a sun lounger on a beach, with Jill St John as 'Ann Archer', in a publicity still for the film, 'Tony Rome', 1967. Directed by Gordon Douglas

The Slow Descent

As the 60s began to head towards the 70s, Sinatra's smooth machine began to splutter. In May 1968, The Wall Street Journal ran a story on Sinatra's links with the Mafia. He who had been paranoid about controlling his life and the press, but could no longer do so. His attempts to stay on top professionally with songs such as "Mrs. Robinson" misfired.

For the first time since 1951 he made no films at all in 1969. This was the year when Mafia man Angelo De Carlo could be heard on an FBI tape talking about Sinatra, about the singer possibly raising funds for a casino, and about how De Carlo had provided Sinatra with women.

1969 was the year the Apollo 10 astronauts orbited the moon and it was the year that Frank's father, Marty, died on January 24th at the age of 74. Frank had flown his father to Texas for heart surgery. It was too late. The loss of Marty was bound to cause a lava flow of pain and emotional hardship for Frank. His father's passing must have made him acutely aware that his own attempts at family life had fallen cruelly short of the mark and that he had deprived his own sons and daughters of the father all children need; one who is there for them at all times. To those around him, he seemed to be a shadow of his former, dynamic self. It was as though the collapse of his marriage to Mia had deflated his spirit, and the liaisons with women thereafter could be limpid affairs that contained none of the spirit of chase and conquer that had once made them crackle and glisten. Sinatra was indeed tired.

The White House still welcomed him; but this time it was a Republican White House; Sinatra had campaigned for the Republicans, and Frank sang in Washington in February 1970 during a tribute to Senator Everett Dirksen.

He was still recording; in 1970 he released Watertown, an acclaimed concept album that Sinatra sang to backing tracks. The public were not convinced and bought just 30,000 copies. He made a film that year, in which he played the title role. Dirty Dingus Magee was another film that sank like a stone and it was his last movie for another ten years. There was a cameo role in an American sitcom, Make Room for Grandaddy. It wasn't hard for Frank to see that the end of his career was lurking just around the corner.

Neither had the Mafia gone away. The organization reared its hydra head again when Sinatra was asked by Joe Colombo, head of one of five crime families in New York, to perform at a rally for the Italian American Civil Rights League, which was dripping with organised crime members; to his credit, Sinatra refused. For his impudence, he was told that if he set foot east of the Mississippi it would be the last step that he ever took. It is no smear on Sinatra's character to say that this threat reduced him to tears of fear. The hit was cancelled when he finally agreed to perform at Madison Square Garden for the league's next large-scale event.

When Mario Puzo's hugely successful The Godfather was filmed, Sinatra tried to get one character, who was undoubtedly based upon himself, taken out of the film script. It was none other than Sam Giancana who told Frank in so many words to butt out. Later, Sinatra met the author by accident and started to scream insanely at Puzo, threatening, as he had so many others, to beat hell out of him.

But was he growing tired of screaming, of the confrontations and assaults on his integrity, as he saw it? Tired of the struggle with himself, of the constant need to stay ahead as a performer and remain top dog? Was he tired of the constant threat to his life by mobsters, or of feeling the need to carry a gun? Yes, he was tired of all those things. He had attained so much, yet he had not, after all, attained everything he wanted; he had also lost so much. *"He was not (the man) I'd known"*, said one of his friends at the time. The vibrant energy for which he was known, his infallible charm, had faded. Sinatra himself said in a conversation with the journalist Thomas Thompson, *"I've had enough, maybe the public has had enough too"*.

On the 2nd of November 1970 he went into the studio to record his final song for Reprise Records. It was entitled "The Game Is over".

Frank Sinatra was 55 years old and had been in show business for 36 of those years. He received a special Oscar early in 1971 in acknowledgement of his work for charity. In April he wrote a press announcement stating that he would retire and that it would be final. On the 13th of June that year, during a fundraising concert for the Motion Picture and TV Relief Fund In Hollywood, the greater part of

his glittering career was indeed, over, for there, in front of a star-studded audience that included Jimmy Stewart, David Niven, Clint Eastwood, Carrie Grant, and Jack Benny, and, appropriately, the President of the United States, Sinatra announced his retirement.

And, for a while, he remained true to his vow never to open his mouth to sing again.

He certainly didn't need to work; he was as wealthy as Croesus and as unable to sustain a relationship as ever. He had been seeing the actress Lois Nettleton since the beginning of the year of 1971, and by the autumn, Sinatra had once again decided that he had found 'the one', and asked her to marry him. Within the hour, he was screaming at her in the street because she had dared, without thinking, to make

him wait for her in front of everybody else. The relationship was over; Frank's ego triumphed over everything.

In 1973, he was asked to perform at a White House reception for the Italian Prime Minister at the request of Richard Nixon, and he did so in April, singing ten songs. He was now firmly in the Republican camp, despite professing a lifelong support for the Democrats, and harboured secret ambitions to an ambassadorship. Which proved that Sinatra was still wrapped in self-deception. And if, as Shirley MacLaine claimed, he had switched sides at the behest of the mob, he was still wrapped up in obligations there, too.

Above: Sinatra, with his minders and his stand in (who is wearing an identical outfit to Sinatra), arriving at Miami beach while filming, 'The Lady In Cement'

Above: Frank Sinatra Palm Springs

Opposite Page: Sinatra family Portrait. L-R Tina Sinatra,
Frank Sinatra (top) Frank Sinatra, Jr. (bottom) Nancy Sinatra

Above: performing on stage

Let's Try That Again

Retirement did not suit Sinatra; he was bored. He missed singing; he missed the adulation. It wasn't possible for him to admit as much, of course, and he could soon be heard saying that the idea of Frank Sinatra retiring was *"a figment of somebody's imagination"*. Frank never could admit to anything that didn't accord with his version of the truth.

By 1973, aged 58, retirement forgotten, his voice no longer so smooth, and *"puffier, rounder in the jaw"* as the Los Angeles Times remarked, Sinatra was back in the public eye with an hour-long television special and an album; Ol' Blue Eyes Is Back. It was immediately successful, rising to number 13 in the Billboard chart. Another accolade arrived; the Songwriter's of America named Frank Sinatra as Entertainer of the Century.

With the bit between his teeth, Sinatra began touring in America and abroad. Sadly, the old Sinatra was travelling alongside and the unpleasantness, the abuse, the paranoia, were back in force. They made him few friends; *"... I think you're the best male vocalist that ever lived, but I also think you're a miserable failure as a human being"*, said the critic from the Boston Globe, George Frazier.

Sinatra was still looking for a woman who would stay with him, and in 1974, an event took place that was to be of great significance to Sinatra's future life; Zeppo Marx, youngest of the famous Marx Brothers troop, and his wife Barbara got divorced. Sinatra had known Barbara since the 60s, and by the time of the divorce she was being seen constantly at Frank's side. Even so, he was still taunted by the idea of Ava, still met her, still asked her to come back to him... and even dallied with the idea of reuniting with his first wife, Nancy; anything to keep the black, lonely emptiness at bay, if only he did not have to look inside himself for redemption.

Frank continued to appear on stage, at Caesar's Place in January, for example, where the manager had pulled a gun on him in 1970 after an argument, and in October of 1974, he starred at Madison Square Garden in New York for a televised concert that later became an album, released under the title The Main Event Live. It was a moderate success and preceded a European tour.

Throughout 1975, he toured America extensively, appearing with such greats as Ella Fitzgerald and also doing concerts in England, Israel and Iran. He became friends with John Denver late that year at Lake Tahoe, where their separate shows at Harrah's sold out. Denver subsequently appeared on Sinatra's TV special Sinatra and Friends.

Still searching for the elusive stability that he desperately hoped someone else could give him, he presented Barbara with a ring in the spring of 1976 as a marriage proposal without saying the words *"will you marry me"*. She was 49 he was 60, and the marriage took place on the 11th of July. The gifts they exchanged were a peacock blue Rolls Royce from him and a green Jaguar from her.

He seemed happy in his new marriage. Nine months later he commented that it had bestowed a *"kind of wonderful tranquility"* upon him, a remarkable statement in the light of his life up until that time. Had he at last found even some of the peace that he desired? *"I live my life in certain ways that I could never change for a woman"*, he has been quoted as saying. Some things didn't change; his generosity to his ex-wives, whom he supported financially. And the womanising? The drinking? His new wife would avoid the questions and any other awkward ones. She was happy; in her own words, *"He was always so sweet and so adorable to me and he made me feel fulfilled. I had everything that I wanted and needed"*.

He continued performing his concerts; ninety-two in nine months. He wanted to keep working until *"I just cannot work any more"*, as he told one interviewer, and that he did, using his Las Vegas shows as the springboard for other concerts.

There was one event in 1977 that did change Sinatra, an event that left *"... a vast void of love"* as his daughter Nancy wrote, *"That made him "a different man"*.

Frank had charted a plane for Dolly, and she was on her way to see her son perform in Las Vegas when the chartered jet smashed into the side of Mount San Gorgonio near Palm Springs. Sinatra was beside himself with grief. He was so much his mother's son, had carried her treatment of him with him throughout his life, his character forged on the anvil of her uncompromising upbringing; and now she had left him.

Alone again.

And alone he would sit for hours without uttering a word.

His daughter Nancy said in 1995 that after that crash he rarely talked about his childhood anymore, as though that part of his life had also left him forever, along with his mother.

There was yet one more major musical success; it came in 1978 when he sang the song **New York, New York** at a charity event. Although it had been the theme song from a movie released the previous year, it now became inextricably linked with Frank Sinatra and its popularity has continued to the present day.

The following year, 1979, he celebrated 40 years in show business, and the celebrations were crowned with a Grammy Trustees Award. His 64th birthday arrived, though he showed no sign of wanting to stop, giving pleasure to audiences from the Egyptian desert to the Royal Albert Hall in England, and from Brazil to California.

As his marriage settled into its defined routines and Sinatra aged, a different, more restrained man came to the fore. His vibrant energies that could turn in a flash to aggression had subsided; he had apparently moderated his drinking, and his wife began to filter those who had access to him. Had she tamed him, or had the old Sinatra simply shuffled off to a quiet place in his and everyone else's memory? Was he too tired to fight anymore, taking an easier route now and allowing his last marriage partner to slowly take over the reigns of his existence? There were arguments. Problems. There was even a separation, briefly. But life alone no longer held any enticements for an ageing man.

A new decade arrived, the 1980s, with Sinatra still there where he felt most at home; on stage, performing. Full of enthusiasm, he started the New Year with another statistical record; this time for the number of people attending a solo performer concert; 175,000 in Rio de Janeiro in January. In March, he released his album Trilogy: Past, Present and Future, containing songs evoking the three eras, which brought in six Grammy nominations and rose to number 17 in the Billboard 200 chart. True to form, when Jonathan Schwartz, a radio show host, dared to criticise the *"Future"* section, describing it as *"... a shocking embarrassment"*, Sinatra's complaint was swift to arrive and his retribution harsh; he ensured that Schwartz was suspended from his job.

The year also brought Frank's first film role for ten years, as Sergeant Edward Delaney in The First Deadly Sin. It was produced by Sinatra and starred himself with Faye Dunaway as his co-star. It was not a box office success, even though some of the critics were kind; *"Sinatra in good form in one of his better serious vehicles"*, was one reviewer's opinion.

The reception for the album he released in 1981, She Shot Me down,

gave him pause for thought. It was considered an artistic success, a triumph even, and he would incorporate one of the melodies from the album into his concerts from then on. Commercially, however, it failed to catch fire.

A pause for thought might also have come when he was chosen in 1983 as a recipient for the Kennedy Centre Honours. Ironically, it was a Republican president, Ronald Reagan, who presented the eulogy for Sinatra. He had, said Reagan, *"... spent his life casting a magnificent and powerful shadow"*.

Indeed he had; in more ways than one.

Although he couldn't know it of course, Frank was doing a lot of things for the last time. In 1984 he went into the studio in April and May to record his last solo album, L. A. Is My Lady, with arrangements by Quincy Jones. It rose to number 8 in the Top Jazz Albums chart. His fans were still out there, still happy to listen to him.

Reagan was there to award him America's highest civilian award in 1985; the Medal of Freedom. It was the year of his 70th birthday.

Sinatra was still powering onwards. Yet thoughts of stopping were slipping through his mind even now as he bathed in more success. The passing years were taking more and more of his contemporaries and important people in his life chronicle, away from him; Yul Brynner, Nelson Riddle, Orson Welles, Harry James. He was aware of his own ageing body and especially his voice, which had been a cause for concern over the last few years as it began to show signs of wear and tear from a lifetime of drinking, smoking, shouting and singing. One year later he was in hospital with an abscess on his large intestine and a major surgical operation lasting 7 ½ hours.

Two weeks later he was back on tour.

And there was an epic tour in 1988, when the old Rat Pack members, Dean Martin, Sammy Davis Jr. and Frank Sinatra got together for what would prove to be the Rat Pack's last hurrah. The constellation of the three ageing stars lasted precisely four days, before angry shouts from the dressing room heralded Dean Martin's departure from the tour. Frank wanted to recreate his through-the-night lifestyle of earlier years, but the old days could not be reconstructed. Liza Minnelli came along to fill in the gap. Having reconnected on the tour, however, Davis and Sinatra often got together over the next two years for concerts. Theirs was a short-lived flourish. For Sinatra there were difficult years ahead. They began in 1990; a year of endings. A year of heartbreak.

Above: Sinatra performing on stage, 1975

Above: performing with Sammy Davis Jr and Liza Minnelli at a 'Rat Pack' reunion concert

We Had
Good Times,
Didn't We?

Barely had the year started, it was the 25th of January, when news came that Ava Gardner had been found dead in bed in her London apartment at the age of 67. The love of a lifetime, the woman to whom he had sent a huge bouquet of flowers every year on her birthday, had ceased to inhabit, to glow in his world. Almost impossible to describe what Frank Sinatra now felt.

The show had to go on; next day, apparently *"... confused, distraught"* as one person remembered, he played to an audience of 18,000 in New York.

He was not long spared the whip; in February, Jimmy Van Heusen died at the age of 77, and in May, having initially refused to undergo surgery for throat cancer that might have saved his life but taken away his voice, Sammy Davis Jr. passed away at the age of 64. Sinatra's daughter Nancy went to see the singer, affectionately known as Smokey, just before he died. Her father was bereft and mourned for the man he had helped so caringly, knowing that he would *"... miss him forever"*.

Another finality, then, as the year drew to a close; a final performance with Ella Fitzgerald took place when he was given an award by the Society of Singers in Los Angeles in December.

Sinatra did what he did best to keep at bay the pangs of loneliness, to distract himself from the messages of an ageing body, failing hearing and cataracts in his eyes; he sang. The voice, too, was failing; *"... in a state of grand deterioration"*, said the Times newspaper in London. For years now, his memory had refused to obey him, and there were many occasions when he forgot the lyrics to the songs that he had been singing for years. A veritable mountain of pills allowed him to keep going, pills ranging from anti-depressants through to sleeping pills. No one new, except his wife, whether the pills were causing his disorientation, his mental confusion and unsteadiness, or helping to prevent them from worsening. Barbara confessed to never leaving his side. He failed to recognise people he knew, and his doctor confirmed what many people had been thinking for some time; he was suffering from *"some degree of dementia"*.

Yet through it all, he sang on, and the fans came to hear him. He sang in America and he sang abroad, and he sang on an album called **Duets**, which was issued in October 1993. Frank recorded by himself, and then other illustrious singers, Tony Bennett, Carly Simon, and Aretha Franklin, added their voices. The album reached number 2 on the Billboard chart. It sold more copies than any other Frank Sinatra album.

In 1994 he was awarded the Legend Award at the 1994 Grammy Awards in March. Later that month he collapsed on stage. It was almost the end of the road. That loomed up in December when he made his final public appearance, in Japan. He had bravely pushed himself to the limit. Now he could give no more.

He became the last surviving member of the legendary Rat Pack trio when Dean Martin bowed out on Christmas Day 1995 aged 78.

The horizons of his world had contracted now. His beloved train set was auctioned off once Barbara had decided that Frank should leave the house he had owned for 40 years at Palm Springs. The move, of course, devastated him, and at his new home in Beverly Hills, he was heard to ask his wife *"when are we going home?"*. He missed the desert. There were tensions between his daughters and Barbara. Shortly before his 81st birthday he had a heart attack and was suffering from extremely serious lung and heart problems.

With his mobility restricted, Sinatra spent his days in front of the television with old stalwarts such as his former road manager Tony Oppedsiano or the actor Don Rickles, and playing poker with friends, of whom his neighbour in Beverly Hills, Jack Lemmon, was one.

But he was aware of and unhappy about his physical and mental condition. It wasn't the way he had envisaged the last years of his life.

On the 14th of May 1998, he was having difficulty breathing and complained to his nurse about chest pains. And then he suffered another heart attack and was rushed to hospital.

As had happened always in the life of Frank Sinatra, so the truth in those last moments of his life was buried in myth creation. The doctors tried to revive him, tried to keep him alive for an hour and a half. No one alerted his daughters.

"Don Quixote tilting at windmills", as Humphrey Bogart had once described him, went into battle one last time.

At 10.50, The Voice finally went quiet forever.

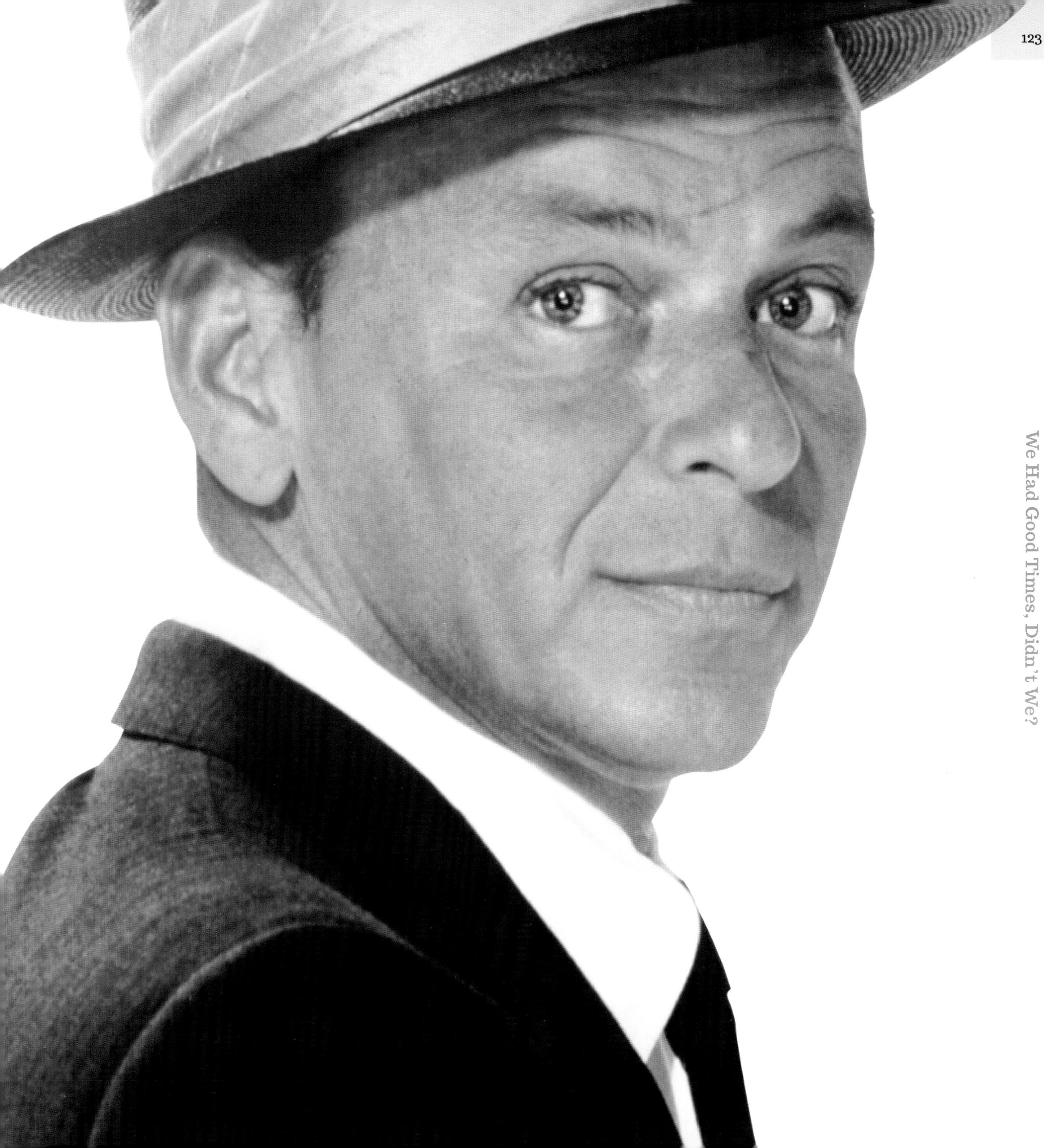

Epilogue

Frank Sinatra was a conundrum wrapped inside a layer of contradictions, a man unleashed from many of the ethical guidelines that much of humanity voluntarily travels with to keep it from reverting to the law of the jungle; perhaps only those in the underworld live so loosely connected to those guidelines; perhaps that was what attracted him to their company. His own untethered behaviour led to violent outbursts throughout his life that included assaults on anyone who dared to question his actions or words. In turn, he was a man assaulted by his own demons and their whiplashing, intense depressions that never released their ironclad grip around his mind. He was never freed by them to relax into a peaceful relationship with the world around him, one that might then have helped him to achieve emotional maturity. He was so profoundly caught up in his own image of himself that to attack that image was to attack his very soul, or so it seemed to him. The consequences could be dire. His valet of fifteen years, George Jacobs, was instantly dismissed without compensation when Frank heard that George had danced with Mia Farrow.

Desperate for long term companionship, he proved totally incapable of taming the one woman he loved above all others, Ava Gardner; his own emotional reservoir was so inadequate that he could not offer her the support she needed; how could he? The tangled, barbed-wire protected ego that nestled inside him needed all the support it could get. They remained friends, nonetheless, for the rest of her life.

For Frank, perhaps a legacy of Italian Catholicism, it seemed that women were either saints or sinners, and he treated them accordingly. Except for one. For most of his life, there had been one woman who had probably meant more to him than even he knew, and she, it appears, never stopped loving him just as she had when they met as young lovers; his first wife, Nancy, who died in September 2004.

The legacy that will be remembered by most, however, is not the temper or the violence, not the unrestrained womanising, nor the dating of famous women such as Judy Garland, Marilyn Monroe, and Angie Dickinson; not the tormented, frustrated man who could not build the world to his liking and struck out in bewilderment and fear. Not even the man who was one of the most famous of those who 'mingled' with the mafiosi. The legacy will be the man with the cheeky smile and blue eyes, and the silky, seductive singing voice that could enchant and bewitch women and make men wish that they were him. It was the golden voice of a generation and a gift from the gods, albeit with a sting embedded in it.

For Frank Sinatra, if that was how it had to be then he would take the sting, sure, why not, you wouldn't feel a thing after a shot of Jack Daniels. But he would fight back as Dolly had taught him so many years before; and he would still sing, sing, sing straight though to the heart of his listeners, right through to the glorious applause and the final curtain.

Frank Sinatra Discography

Studio albums at Columbia

1946 The voice of Frank Sinatra Released 4/¾6 1 (US)

1947 Songs by Sinatra Released 4/47 2 (US)

1948 Christmas Songs by Sinatra Released 1948

1949 Frankly Sentimental Released 20/6/49

1950 Dedicated to You Released 03/50

1950 Sing and Dance with Frank Sinatra Released 16/10/50

Albums at Capitol

1954 Songs for Young Lovers Released 01/54 3 (US)

1954 Swing Easy! Released 02/8/54 3 (US) 5 (UK)

1955 in the Wee Small Hours Released 04/55 2 (US) RIAA Gold

1956 Songs for Swinging Lovers! Released 03/56 2 (US) 1 (UK) RIAA Gold

1956 Close to You Released 01/57 5 (US) To (UK)

1956 A Swingin' Affair! Released 06/57 7 (US) 1 (UK)

1957 Where Are You? Released 09/57 3 (US)

1957 A Jolly Christmas from Frank Sinatra Released 09/57 18 (US) RIAA Platinum

1958 Come Fly with Me Released 01/58 1 (US) 2 (UK) RIAA Gold

1958 Frank Sinatra Sings for Only the Lonely Released 09/58 1 (US) 5 (UK) RIAA Gold

1959 Come Dance with Me! Released 01/59 2 (US) 2 (UK) RIAA Gold

1959 No One Cares Released 07/59 7 (US)

1960 Nice 'n' Easy Released 07/16 1 (US) 4 (UK) RIAA Gold

1961 Sinatra Swinging Session!!! Released 01/61 6 (US) 6 (UK)

1961 Come Swing with Me! Released 07/61 12 (US) 13 (UK)

1962 Point of No Return Released 03/62 18 (US)

1993 Duets Released 02/10/93 2 (US) 5 (UK) 3 x RIAA Platinum, CRIA 2 x Platinum

1994 Duets II Released 15/10/94 9(US) 29 (UK) RIAA Platinum, CRIA Platinum

Reprise Albums

1961 Ring-a-Ding-Ding! Released 03/61 6 (US) 9 (UK)

1961 Swing along with Me (Retitled Sinatra Swings) Released 07/61 6 (US) 8 (UK)

1961 I Remember Tommy Released 10/61 5 (US) 10 (UK)

1962 Sinatra and Strings Released 01/62 8 (US) 6 (UK)

1962 Sinatra and Swingin' Brass Released 07/62 19 (US) 14 (UK)

1962 All Alone Released 10/62 26 (US)

1962 Sinatra Sings Great Songs from Great Britain Released 11/62 12 (UK)

1962 Sinatra-Basie: An Historic Musical First Released 10/12/62 16 (US) 2 (UK)

1963 The Concert Sinatra Released 05/63 11 (US) 8 (UK)

1963 Sinatra Sinatra Released 08/63 8 (US) 7 (UK) RIAA Gold

1963 Sinatra Sings Days of Wine and Roses, Moon River, and Other Academy Award Winners Released 03/64 10 (US)

1963 America, I Hear You Singing (with Bing Crosby and Fred Waring) Released 04/64 116 (US)

1964 It Might As Well Be Swing (with Count Basie) Released 08/64 13 (US) 17 (UK)

1964 12 Songs of Christmas (with Bing Crosby and Fred Waring) Released 08/64

1964 Softly, As I Leave You Released 10/64 19 (US) 20 (UK)

1965 September of My Years Released 08/65 5 (US) RIAA Gold

1965 My Kind of Broadway Released 10/65 30 (US)

1965 A Man and His Music Released 10/65 9 (US) RIAA Platinum

1966 Moonlight Sinatra Released 03/66 34 (US)

1966 Strangers in the Night Released 05/66 1 (US) 4 (UK) RIAA Platinum

1966 That's Life Released 10/66 6 (US) 22 (UK) RIAA Gold

1967 Francis Albert Sinatra and Antonio Carlos Jobim Released 03/67 19 (US)

1967 The World We Knew Released 08/67 24 (US) 28 (UK)

1968 Francis A. and Edward K. (with Duke Ellington) Released 01/68 78 (US)

1968 The Sinatra Family Wish You a Merry Christmas (with His Children) Released 09/68

1968 Cycles Released 10/68 18 (US) RIAA Gold

1969 My Way Released 03/69 11 (US) 2 (UK) RIAA Gold

1969 A Man Alone Released 08/69 30 (US) 18 (UK)

1970 - Watertown - Released 03/70 104 (US) 14 (UK)

1971 Sinatra and Company (with Antonio Carlos Jobim) - Released 03/71 74 (US) 9 (UK)

1973 Ol' Blue Eyes is Back Released 09/73 13 (US) 12 (UK) RIAA Gold

1974 Some Nice Things I've Missed Released 07/74 48 (US) 35 (UK)

1980 Trilogy: Past Present and Future Released 03/80 17 (US) RIAA Gold

1981 She Shot Me Down Released 10/81 52 (US)

Qwest Albums

1984 L.A. Is My Lady Released 08/84 58 (US) 41 (UK)

Compilation Albums

Capitol

1956 This Is Sinatra! Released 10/56 8 (US) 1 (UK) RIAA Gold

1958 This Is Sinatra Volume 2 Released 03/58 8 (US) 3 (UK)

1959 Look to Your Heart Released 04/59 8 (US) 5 (UK)

1959 The Rare Frank Sinatra (Frank Sinatra Album) Released 1959

1961 All The Way Released 03/61 4 (US)

1962 Sinatra Sings of Love and Things Released 07/62 21 (US)

Reprise

1965 Sinatra '65: The Singer Today Released 06/65 9 (US)

1968 Frank Sinatra's Greatest Hits Released 08/68 55 (US) RIAA 2x Platinum

1972 Frank Sinatra's Greatest Hits Vol 2 Released 05/72 88 (US) 5 (UK) RIAA Platinum

1994 The Sinatra Christmas Album Released 11/94

2014 The Sinatra Christmas Collection Released 10/2004

Colombia

1995 16 Most Requested Songs Released 05/95

Laser Light Album

1995 Christmas Through The Years Released 10/95

Live Albums

Reprise

1966 Sinatra at the Sands (with Count Basie) Released 07/66 9 (US) 7 (UK) RIAA Gold

1974 The Main Event Live Released 10/74 37 (US) 30 (UK) RIAA Gold

Post-retirement Albums

1994 Sinatra & Sextet: Live in Paris Released 22/03/94

1995 Sinatra 80th: Live in Concert Released 14/11/95

1997 Frank Sinatra with the Red Norvo Quintet: Live in Australia 1959 Released 06/04/97

1999 Sinatra '57 in Concert Released 06/04/99

2005 Live from Las Vegas (Frank Sinatra Album) 26/04/05

2006 Sinatra: Vegas Released 07/11/06 165 (US)

2009 Live at the Meadowlands Released 05/05/09

2009 Sinatra: New York Released 03/10/09

2011 Best of Vegas Released 08/02/11

Ratpack Albums

1993 Frank Sinatra, Dean Martin, Sammy Davis Jr. At Villa Venice, Chicago Live 1962 Released

1999 Frank, Sammy and Dean: The Summit in Concert Released 1999

2001 The Rat Pack Live at the Sands Released 1999

2002 Ratpack: From Vegas to St. Louis Released 2002

2002 Christmas with the Rat Pack Released 22/10/02

2003 The Ultimate Rat Pack Collection: Live & Swinging' Released 2003

Albums conducted by Frank Sinatra

1946 Frank Sinatra Conducts the Music of Alec Wilder Released 1946

1956 Frank Sinatra Conducts Tone Poems of Color Released 1956

1957 The Man I Love (artist: Peggy Lee) Released March 1957

1958 Sleep War (artist: Dean Martin) Released 02/03/59

1962 Frank Sinatra Conducts Music from Pictures and Plays Released 2011

1982 Syms by Sinatra (artist: Sylvia Syms) Released 1982

1983 What's New (with Charles Turner, trumpeter) Released 1983

Box Sets and Collections

RCA Records

1957 Frank and Tommy (Sinatra/Dorsey)

1988 All Time Greatest Hits, Vols. 1-4 (Sinatra/Dorsey)

1994 The Song Is You (Sinatra/Dorsey)

1996 Frank Sinatra & Tommy Dorsey - Greatest Hits

1998 Frank Sinatra & the Tommy Dorsey Orchestra

2005 The Essential Frank Sinatra with the Tommy Dorsey Orchestra

Columbia Records

1953 Get Happy!

1955 Frankie

1956 The Voice

1956 That Old Feeling

1957 Adventures of the Heart

1957 Christmas Dreaming

1958 Love Is a Kick

1958 The Broadway Kick

1958 Put Your Dreams Away

1958 The Frank Sinatra Story in Music

1959 Come Back to Sorrento

1966 Greatest Hits: The Early Years

1966 Greatest Hits: The Early Years Volume Two

1968 Someone to Watch Over Me

1968 In Hollywood 1943-1949

1972 In The Beginning: 1943 To 1951

1986 The Voice: The Columbia Years (1943-1952)

1987 Hello Young Lovers

1988 Sinatra Rarities: The Columbia Years

1993 The Columbia Years 1943-1952: The Complete Recordings

1994 The Columbia Years 19431952: The V-Discs

1994 The Essence of Frank Sinatra

1995 16 Most Requested Songs

1995 The Complete Recordings Nineteen Thirty-Nine (Harry James & His Orchestra featuring Frank Sinatra)

1995 I've Got a Crush on You

1996 Sinatra Sings Rodgers and Hammerstein

1997 Frank Sinatra Sings His Greatest Hits

1997 Portrait of Sinatra: Columbia Classics

1998 The Best of the Columbia Years: 1943-1952

2000 Super Hits

2001 Love Songs

2003 The Essential Frank Sinatra: The Columbia Years

2003 The Real Complete Columbia Years V-Discs

2003 Sinatra Sings Cole Porter

2003 Sinatra Sings George Gershwin

2007 A Voice in Time: 1939-1952

2009 From the Heart

Capitol Records

1956 This Is Sinatra!

1958 This Is Sinatra Volume 2

1959 Look to Your Heart

1960 Swing Easy

1961 Look Over Your Shoulder

1961 All the Way

1962 The Great Years
1962 Sinatra Sings...of Love and Things
1963 Sinatra Sings the Select Johnny Mercer
1963 Sings Rodgers and Hart
1963 Tell Her You Love Her
1964 The Great Hits of Frank Sinatra
1965 Sings the Select Cole Porter
1966 Forever Frank
1967 Nevertheless I'm in Love With You
1967 Songs for the Young at Heart
1967 The Nearness of You
1967 Try a Little Tenderness
1968 The Best Of Frank Sinatra
1972 The Cole Porter Songbook
1972 The Great Years
1974 One More for the Road
1974 Round # 1
1988 Screen Sinatra
1989 The Capitol Collectors Series
1990 The Capitol Years
1992 Concepts
1992 The Best of the Capitol Years
1995 Sinatra 80th: All the Best
1996 The Complete Capitol Singles Collection
1998 The Capitol Years (21-Disc, UK)
2000 Classic Sinatra: His Greatest Performances 1953-1960
2002 Classic Duets
2007 Romance: Songs From the Heart
2008 Sinatra at the Movies
2009 Classic Sinatra II
2011 Sinatra: Best of the Best

Reprise Records

1965 Sinatra '65: The Singer Today
1965 A Man and His Music
1965 My Kind of Broadway
1966 A Man and His Music (Part II): The Frank Sinatra CBS Television Special
1968 Frank Sinatra's Greatest Hits
1972 Frank Sinatra's Greatest Hits, Vol. 2
1977 Portrait of Sinatra - Forty Songs from the Life of a Man
1979 Sinatra-Jobim Sessions
1983 New York New York: His Greatest Hits
1990 The Reprise Collection
1991 Sinatra Reprise: The Very Good Years
1992 Sinatra: Soundtrack To The CBS Mini-Series
1994 The Sinatra Christmas Album
1995 The Complete Reprise Studio Recordings

1996 Everything Happens to Me
1997 The Very Best of Frank Sinatra
1997 My Way: The Best of Frank Sinatra
1998 Lucky Numbers
2000 Reprise Musical Repertory Theatre
2002 Frank Sinatra in Hollywood 1940-1964
2002 Greatest Love Songs
2004 Frank Sinatra Christmas Collection
2004 Romance
2008 Nothing but the Best

LaserLight

1995 Christmas Through the Years

Rhino Records

2009 Seduction: Sinatra Sings of Love

Star Mark Compilations

2008 Frank Sinatra's Greatest Hits

Shout! Factory

2010 Frank Sinatra: Concert Collection

Starlite

1993 Frank Sinatra, Dean Martin, Sammy Davis Jr: Rat Pack is Back

Singles

1939

• From the Bottom of My Heart / Melancholy Mood (Brunswick Records)
• Its Funny to Everyone but Me (by Jack Lawrence) / Vol Visto Gailey Star (by Jack Palmer)
• Here Comes the Night / Feet Draggin' Blues (instrumental)
• My Buddy / Willow Weep For Me (instrumental)
• On a Little Street in Singapore / Who Told You I Cared?
• Ciribiribin / Avalon (instrumental)

1940

• Every Day of My Life / Cross Country Jump (instrumental)
• All or Nothing at All / Flash (instrumental) (re-issued 1943)
• With the Tommy Dorsey Orchestra (RCA Victor) (1940-1942)

1940

• Too Romantic / Sweet Potato Piper (by The Pied Pipers)
• The Sky Fell Down / What Can I Say After I Say I'm Sorry? (by The Pied Pipers)
• Shake Down the Stars / Moments in the Moonlight
• Say It (Over and Over Again) / My, My (by The Pied Pipers)

- Polka Dots and Moonbeams / I'll Be Seeing You
- The Fable of the Rose / This Is the Beginning of the End
- Imagination / Charming Little Faker (by The Pied Pipers)
- Devil May Care / Fools Rush In (Where Angels Fear to Tread)
- It's a Lovely Day Tomorrow / You're Lonely and I'm Lonely
- April Played the Fiddle / I Haven't Time to be a Millionaire
- Yours Is My Heart Alone / Hear My Song Violetta
- I'll Never Smile Again (with The Pied Pipers) / Marcheta (instrumental)
- All This and Heaven Too / Where Do You Keep Your Heart?
- East of the Sun (and West of the Moon) / Head on My Pillow
- And So Do I (by Connie Haines) / The One I Love
  (Belongs to Somebody Else) (with The Pied Pipers)
- Only Forever (by Allan Storr) / Trade Winds
- Love Lies / The Call Of The Canyon
- Whispering / Funny Little Pedro (by The Pied Pipers)
- I Could Make You Care / The World Is In My Arms
- Our Love Affair / That's for Me (by Connie Haines)
- Looking for Yesterday / I Wouldn't Take a Million (by Connie Haines)
- We Three (My Echo, My Shadow, and Me) / Tell Me at Midnight
- You're Breaking My Heart All Over Again / Shadows on the Sand
- Two Dreams Met (by Connie Haines) / When You Awake
- I'd Know You Anywhere / You've Got Me This Way (by The Pied Pipers)
- Do You Know Why? / Isn't That Just Like Love? (by The Pied Pipers)
- Anything / Another One of Them Things
- You Say The Sweetest Things (by Connie Haines and The Pied Pipers) / Not So Long Ago
- Stardust (with The Pied Pipers) / Swanee River (instrumental)

1941

- Oh! Look at Me Now (with Connie Haines and The Pied Pipers) / You Might Have Belonged To Another
- Dolores (with The Pied Pipers) / I Tried
- Do I Worry? (with The Pied Pipers) / Little Man With A Candy Cigar (by Jo Stafford)
- Without a Song / Deep River (instrumental)
- It's Always You / Birds of a Feather (by Connie Haines)
- You're Dangerous (by Connie Haines) / You Lucky People You
- Everything Happens to Me / Watcha Know Joe (by Jo Stafford and The Pied Pipers)
- Let's Get Away from It All (with Jo Stafford, Connie Haines and The Pied Pipers)
- Kiss the Boys Goodbye (by Connie Haines) / I'll Never Let a Day Pass By
- Love Me As I Am / Nine Old Men (by The Pied Pipers)
- Neiani / This Love of Mine (with The Pied Pipers)
- I Guess I'll Have to Dream the Rest (with The Pied Pipers) / Loose Lid Special (instrumental)
- You And I / Free for All (with The Pied Pipers)
- Blue Skies / Backstage At The Ballet (instrumental)
- Pale Moon (An Indian Love Song) / Hallelujah
- Two In Love / A Sinner Kissed An Angel
- Embraceable You (by Jo Stafford) / The Sunshine of Your Smile
- Violets for Your Furs / Somebody Loves Me (by The Pied Pipers)

- I Think of You / Who Can I Turn To? (by Jo Stafford)
- It Isn't a Dream Anymore / How Do You Do Without Me?

1942

- Winter Weather (by The Pied Pipers) / How About You?
- The Last Call for Love / Poor You (by The Pied Pipers)
- I'll Take Tallulah (with Jo Stafford, Tommy Dorsey and The Pied Pipers) / Not So Quiet Please (instrumental)
- (You're a) Snootie Little Cutie (with Connie Haines and The Pied Pipers) / Moonlight on the Ganges (instrumental)
- Somewhere a Voice is Calling / Well Git It (instrumental)
- Just As Though You Were Here / The Street of Dreams (with The Pied Pipers)
- Be Careful, It's My Heart / Take Me
- He's My Guy (by Jo Stafford) / Light a Candle in the Chapel
- A Boy In Khaki, A Girl In Lace (by Jo Stafford) / In the Blue of Evening
- There Are Such Things / Daybreak (with The Pied Pipers)
- Night and Day / The Night We Called It a Day
- The Lamplighters Serenade / The Song Is You

1943

- Close to You / You'll Never Know
- Sunday, Monday, or Always / If You Please
- People Will Say Were in Love / Oh, What a Beautiful Mornin'

1944

- I Couldn't Sleep a Wink Last Night / A Lovely Way to Spend an Evening (with The Bobby Tucker Singers)
- White Christmas (with The Bobby Tucker Singers) / If You Are But a Dream
- Saturday Night (Is the Loneliest Night of the Week) / I Dream of You (More than You Dream I Do)

1945

- What Makes the Sunset? / I Begged Her
- Ol' Man River / Stormy Weather (with The Ken Lane Singers)
- I Should Care / When Your Lover Has Gone
- Dream / There's No You
- Put Your Dreams Away (For Another Day) / If You are But a Dream (reissue)
- Homesick That's All / A Friend of Yours (with The Ken Lane Singers)
- If I Loved You / You'll Never Walk Alone (with The Ken Lane Singers)
- The Charm of You / I Fall in Love Too Easily
- My Shawl / Stars In Your Eyes (with the Xavier Cugat Orchestra)
- Lily Belle / Don't Forget Tonight Tomorrow (with The Charioteers)
- White Christmas (reissue) / Mighty Lak' a Rose
- Nancy (With the Laughing Face) / The Cradle Song
- America the Beautiful (with The Ken Lane Singers) / The House I Live In

1946

- Oh! What It Seemed to Be / Day by Day
- Full Moon and Empty Arms / You are too Beautiful
- All Through the Day / Two Hearts are Better Than One
- They Say It's Wonderful / The Girl That I Marry
- From This Day Forward / Something Old, Something New
- Soliloquy (Part 1 & 2)
- Five Minutes More / How Cute Can You Be?
- One Love / Somewhere In The Night
- Begin the Beguine / Where Is My Bess?
- The Coffee Song / The Things We Did Last Summer
- Silent Night (with The Ken Lane Singers) / Adeste Fideles
- Jingle Bells (with The Ken Lane Singers) / White Christmas (reissue)
- September Song (8) / Among My Souvenirs

1947

- This Is the Night / Hush-A-Bye Island
- That's How Much I Love You (with The Page Cavanaugh Trio) / I Got A Gal I Love (In North and South Dakota)
- I Want to Thank Your Folks / Why Shouldn't It Happen to Us?
- Its the Same Old Dream (with Four Hits and a Miss) / The Brooklyn Bridge
- Sweet Lorraine / Nat Meets June (by Nat King Cole and June Christy)
- I Believe / Time after Time
- Mamselle / Stella by Starlight
- Almost Like Being in Love / There But For You Go I
- Tea for Two / My Romance (with Dinah Shore)
- Aintcha Ever Comin' Back / I Have But One Heart
- Christmas Dreaming (A Little Early This Year) / The Stars Will Remember
- I've Got a Home In That Rock / Jesus Is a Rock (In a Weary Land) (with The Charioteers)
- So Far / A Fellow Needs a Girl
- The Dum Dot Song (with The Pied Pipers) / It All Came True (with Alvy West and the Little Band)
- You're My Girl / Can't You Just See Yourself?

1948

- What'll I Do? / My Cousin Louella (With The Tony Mottola Trio)
- But Beautiful / If I Only Had a Match
- For Every Man There's a Woman / I'll Make Up for Everything
- But None Like You / We Just Couldn't Say Goodbye (With The Tony Mottola Trio)
- I've Got a Crush on You (featuring Bobby Hackett) / Ever Homeward
- All of Me / I Went Down to Virginia
- It Only Happens When I Dance With You / A Fella With an Umbrella
- Nature Boy (with The Jeff Alexander Choir) / S'posin (With The Tony Mottola Trio)
- Just for Now / Everybody Loves Somebody

1949

- Kiss Me Again / My Melancholy Baby

- Autumn in New York / (Once Upon) A Moonlight Night
- Señorita / If I Steal a Kiss
- A Little Learnin' Is a Dangerous Thing (Part 1 & 2) (with Pearl Bailey)
- Sunflower / Once In Love With Amy
- Why Can't You Behave? (with The Phil Moore Four) / No Orchids For My Lady
- Comme Ci Comme Ca / While the Angelus Was Ringing
- If You Stub Your Toe on the Moon (with The Phil Moore Four) / When Is Sometime?
- Bop! Goes My Heart (with The Phil Moore Four) / Where Is the One?
- Some Enchanted Evening / Bali Hai
- The Right Girl for Me / Night After Night
- The Hucklebuck (with The Ken Lane Quintet) / It Happens Every Spring
- Let's Take an Old Fashioned Walk (with Doris Day and The Ken Lane Singers) / Just One Way To Say I Love You
- It All Depends on You / I Only Have Eyes for You (with The Ken Lane Singers)
- Don't Cry Joe (with The Pastels) / The Wedding of Lili Marlene
- Bye Bye Baby (with The Pastels) / Just a Kiss Apart
- If I Ever Love Again (with The Double Daters) / Every Man Should Marry
- That Lucky Old Sun / Could'ja? (with The Pied Pipers)
- Mad About You / (On the Island of) Stromboli
- The Old Master Painter (with The Modernaires) / Lost in the Stars

1950

- Sorry / Why Remind Me? (with The Modernaires)
- (We've Got a) Sure Thing (with The Modernaires) / Sunshine Cake (with Paula Kelly)
- Chattanoogie Shoe Shine Boy / Gods Country (with The Jeff Alexander Choir)
- Kisses and Tears (with Jane Russell and The Modernaires) / When the Sun Goes Down
- American Beauty Rose (with Mitch Millers Dixieland Band) / Just An Old Stone House
- Poinciana (Song of the Tree) / There's No Business Like Show Business
- Peachtree Street (with Rosemary Clooney) / This is the Night (reissue)
- Goodnight, Irene (with The Mitch Miller Singers) / My Blue Heaven
- Life Is So Peculiar (with Helen Carroll and The Swantones) / Dear Little Boy of Mine (with The Mitch Miller Singers)
- One Finger Melody / Accidents Will Happen
- Nevertheless (I'm in Love with You) / I Guess Ill Have to Dream the Rest (with The Whippoorwills)
- Let It Snow! Let It Snow! Let It Snow! (with The Swanson Quartet) / Remember Me In Your Dreams (with The Whippoorwills)

1951

- I Am Loved / You Don't Remind Me
- Take My Love / Come Back to Sorrento
- Love Means Love / Cherry Pies Ought to Be You (with Rosemary Clooney)
- You're the One (for Me) / Faithful (with The Skylarks)
- We Kiss in a Shadow / Hello Young Lovers
- Love Me / I Whistle a Happy Tune
- Mama Will Bark (with Dagmar) / I'm a Fool to Want You (14)
- It's a Long Way From Your House to My House / I Fall In Love With You Ev'ry Day

- Castle Rock / Deep Night (with Harry James and his Orchestra)
- April in Paris / London by Night

1952

- I Hear a Rhapsody / I Could Write a Book (with The Jeff Alexander Choir)
- Feet of Clay / Don't Ever Be Afraid to Go Home
- My Girl / Walkin' in the Sunshine
- Luna Rossa (Blushing Moon) (with The Norman Luboff Choir) / Tennessee Newsboy
- Bim Bam Baby / Azure-Te (Paris Blues)
- The Birth of the Blues / Why Try to Change Me Now?
- I'm Glad There Is You / You Can Take My Word for It Baby (with The Page Cavanaugh Trio)

1953

- Shelia (with The Jeff Alexander Choir) / Day by Day (reissue)
- I'm Walking Behind You / Lean Baby
- I've Got the World on a String / My One and Only Love
- From Here to Eternity / Anytime, Anywhere
- South of the Border (Down Mexico Way) / I Love You

1954

- I'm a Fool to Want You (reissue) / If I Forget You
- Young at Heart / Take a Chance
- Don't Worry 'bout Me / I Could Have Told You
- Three Coins in the Fountain / Rain (Falling From the Skies)
- The Gal That Got Away / Half as Lovely (Twice as True)
- It Worries Me / When I Stop Loving You
- The Christmas Waltz / White Christmas
- You, My Love / Someone to Watch Over Me
- I'm a Fool to Want You (reissue) / If I Forget You

1955

- Melody of Love / I'm Gonna Live Till I Die (with Ray Anthony and his Orchestra)
- Why Should I Cry Over You? / Don't Change Your Mind About Me (with June Hutton and the Pied Pipers)
- Two Hearts, Two Kisses (Make One Love) / From the Bottom to the Top (with The Nuggets and Big Dave's Music)
- Learnin' the Blues / If I Had Three Wishes
- Not as a Stranger / How Could You Do a Thing Like That to Me?
- Same Old Saturday Night / Fairy Tale
- Love and Marriage / The Impatient Years
- (Love Is) The Tender Trap / Weep They Will

1956

- Flowers Mean Forgiveness / You'll Get Yours
- (How Little It Matters) How Little We Know / Five Hundred Guys
- You're Sensational / Wait for Me (theme from Johnny Concho)
- True Love (by Bing Crosby and Grace Kelly) / Well, Did You Evah! (with Bing Crosby)

- Mind if I Make Love to You? / Who Wants to Be a Millionaire? (with Celeste Holm)
- Hey! Jealous Lover / You Forgot All the Words
- Can I Steal a Little Love? / Your Love for Me

1957

- Crazy Love / So Long, My Love
- You're Cheatin' Yourself (If You're Cheatin' On Me) / Something Wonderful Happens In Summer
- All the Way / Chicago (That Toddlin' Town)
- Witchcraft / Tell Her You Love Her
- Mistletoe and Holly / The Christmas Waltz (with The Ralph Brewster Singers)

1958

- Nothing In Common / How are Ya Fixed for Love? (with Keely Smith)
- Monique (from Kings Go Forth) / Same Old Song and Dance
- Mr. Success / Sleep Warm
- To Love and Be Loved / No One Ever Tells You

1959

- French Foreign Legion / Time After Time
- High Hopes (with A Bunch o' Kids) / All My Tomorrows
- Talk to Me / They Came to Cordura

1960

- It's Nice to Go Trav'ling
- River, Stay Way from My Door / It's Over, It's Over, It's Over
- Nice 'N' Easy / This Was My Love
- Old MacDonald / You'll Always Be the One I Love

1961

- My Blue Heaven / Sentimental Baby
- American Beauty Rose / Sentimental Journey
- The Second Time Around / Tina
- Granada / The Curse of an Aching Heart
- I'll Be Seeing You / The One I Love (Belongs to Somebody Else)
- Imagination / It's Always You
- I'm Getting Sentimental Over You / East of the Sun (and West of the Moon)
- There Are Such Things / Polka Dots and Moonbeams
- Without a Song / It Started All Over Again
- Take Me / Daybreak
- Pocketful of Miracles / Name It and It's Yours
- The Coffee Song
- Ring-a-Ding-Ding! / Nothing but the Best

1962

- I've Heard That Song Before / The Moon Was Yellow
- I'll Remember April / Five Minutes More

• I Love Paris / Hidden Persuasion

Reprise singles (1961-1983)

• Stardust / Come Rain or Come Shine
• Ev'rybody's Twistin' / Nothin' but the Best
• Goody Goody / Love Is Just Around the Corner
• The Look of Love / I Left My Heart in San Francisco
• The Look of Love / Indiscreet
• Me and My Shadow (with Sammy Davis, Jr.) / Sam's Song
  (by Sammy Davis, Jr. and Dean Martin)

1963

• Call Me Irresponsible / Tina (reissue)
• I Have Dreamed / Come Blow Your Horn
• A New Kind of Love / Love Isn't Just for the Young
• Fugue for Tinhorns / The Oldest Established (with Dean Martin and Bing Crosby)
• Have Yourself a Merry Little Christmas / How Shall I Send Thee? (by Les Baxter's Balladeers)

1964

• Stay with Me (Theme from The Cardinal) / Talk to Me Baby
• My Kind of Town / I Like to Lead When I Dance
• Softly, as I Leave You / Then Suddenly Love
• Hello Dolly (with Count Basie)
• I Heard the Bells on Christmas Day / The Little Drummer Boy
  (with Fred Waring & His Pennsylvanians)
• We Wish You the Merriest / Go Tell It On the Mountain
  (with Bing Crosby and Fred Waring & His Pennsylvanians)
• Somewhere in Your Heart / Emily

1965

• Anytime at All / Available
• Tell Her (You Love Her Each Day) / Here's to the Losers
• Forget Domani / I Can't Believe I'm Losing You
• When Somebody Loves You / When I'm Not Near the Girl I Love
• Ev'rybody Has the Right to Be Wrong! / I'll Only Miss Her When I Think of Her
• It Was a Very Good Year / Moment To Moment

1966

• Strangers in the Night / Oh, You Crazy Moon
• Summer Wind / You Make Me Feel So Young (with Count Basie & His Orchestra (live))
• That's Life / September of My Years

1967

• Somethin' Stupid (with Nancy Sinatra) / Give Her Love
• The World We Knew (Over and Over) / You Are There
• This Town / This is My Love

1968

• I Can't Believe I'm Losing You / How Old Am I?
• Cycles / My Way of Life
• Whatever Happened to Christmas / I Wouldn't Trade Christmas (with Frank Sinatra, Jr.,
  Nancy Sinatra and Tina Sinatra)

1969

• Rain in My Heart / Star!
• My Way / Blue Lace
• Love's Been Good to Me / A Man Alone
• Goin' Out of My Head / Forget to Remember
• I Would Be In Love (Anyway) / Watertown
• What's Now Is Now / The Train

1970

• Lady Day / Song of the Sabiá
• Feelin' Kinda Sunday (with Nancy Sinatra) / Kids (by Nancy Sinatra)
• Something / Bein' Green

1971

• Life's a Trippy Thing (with Nancy Sinatra) / I'm Not Afraid
• I Will Drink The Wine / Sunrise In The Morning

1973

• Let Me Try Again / Send in the Clowns
• You Will be My Music / Winners

1974

• Bad, Bad Leroy Brown / I'm Gonna Make It All The Way
• You Turned My World Around / Satisfy Me One More Time

1975

• Anytime (I'll Be There) / The Hurt Doesn't Go Away
• I Believe I'm Gonna Love You / The Only Couple on the Floor
• A Baby Just Like You / Christmas Memories

1976

• The Saddest Thing of All / Empty Tables
• I Sing the Songs (I Write the Songs) / Empty Tables
• Stargazer / The Best I Ever Had (featuring Sam Butera)
• Dry Your Eyes / Like a Sad Song
• I Love My Wife / Send in the Clowns

1977

• Night and Day (disco version) / Everybody Ought to Be in Love

1980

- Theme from New York, New York / That's What God Looks Like to Me
- You and Me (We Wanted It All) / I've Been There!

1981

- Say Hello / Good Thing Going (Going Gone)

1983

- Here's to the Band / It's Sunday (with Tony Mottola)
- To Love a Child / That's What God Looks Like to Me

1984

- Teach Me Tonight / The Best of Everything
- Mack the Knife / It's All Right with Me
- L.A. Is My Lady / Until the Real Thing Comes Along

1986

Only One to a Customer

1986/88

The Girls I never Kissed

1987

When Joanna Loved Me (Live recording)

1988

 Leave it all to Me

1988

My Foolish Head

1988

Bye Bye Blackbird (Live recording

1993

 I've Got You Under My Skin (with Bono)

1994

See the Show Again

1995

Maybe This Time

Frank Sinatra Discography

Frank Sinatra Filmography

Feature Films

1944 Higher and Higher - Himself

1944 Step Lively - Glen Russell

1945 Anchors Aweigh - Clarence "Brooklyn" Doolittle

1945 The House I Live In - Himself

1946 Till the Clouds Roll By - Himself

1947 It Happened in Brooklyn - Danny Webson Miller

1948 The Kissing Bandit - Ricardo

1948 The Miracle of the Bells - Father Paul

1949 Take Me Out to the Ball Game - Dennis Ryan

1949 On the Town - Chip

1951 Double Dynamite - Johnny Dalton

1952 Meet Danny Wilson - Danny Wilson

1953 From Here to Eternity - Pvt. Angelo Maggio (Academy Award for Best Supporting Actor; Golden Globe Award for Best Supporting Actor Motion Picture.)

1954 Young at Heart - Barney Sloan

1954 Suddenly - John Baron

1955 The Man With The Golden Arm - Frankie Machine (Nominated Academy Award for Best Actor; Nominated BAFTA Award for Best Actor in a Leading Role.)

1955 Guys and Dolls - Nathan Detroit

1955 The Tender Trap - Charlie Y. Reader

1955 Not as a Stranger - Alfred Boone (Nominated BAFTA Award for Best Actor in a Leading Role.)

1955 Finian's Rainbow (uncompleted)

1956 High Society - Mike Connor

1956 Johnny Concho - Johnny Concho (aka Johnny Collins.)

1956 Around the World in Eighty Days - cameo as saloon pianist

1956 Carousel - Billy Bigelow (Sinatra recorded two songs, but walked off set having been told that each scene was to be filmed twice. He was replaced by Gordon MacRae.)

1956 Meet Me in Las Vegas - cameo as himself

1957 Pal Joey - Joey Evans (Golden Globe Award for Best Actor Motion Picture Musical or Comedy.)

1957 The Joker Is Wild - Joe E. Lewis ("All the Way" won the Academy Award for Best Original Song.)

1957 The Pride and the Passion - Miguel

1958 Some Came Running - Dave Hirsh

1958 Kings Go Forth - 1st Lt. Sam Loggins

1959 Never so Few - Captain Tom Reynolds

1959 A Hole in the Head - Tony Manetta ("High Hopes" won the Academy Award for Best Original Song.)

1960 Can-Can - François Durnais

1960 Ocean's Eleven - Danny Ocean

1960 Pepe - cameo as himself

1961 The Devil at 4 O'Clock - Harry

1961 The Manchurian Candidate - Capt. / Maj. Bennett Marco

1962 The Road to Hong Kong - The 'Twig' on Plutonium (Uncredited.)

1962 Sergeants 3 - First-Sergeant Mike Merry

1962 4 for Texas - Zack Thomas

1962 Come Blow Your Horn - Alan Baker (Nominated Golden Globe Award for Best Actor Motion Picture Musical or Comedy.)

1962 The List of Adrian Messenger - cameo

1964 Robin and the 7 Hoods - Robbo ("My Kind of Town" was nominated for the Academy Award for Best Original Song.)

1965 Marriage on the Rocks - Dan Edwards

1965 Von Ryan's Express - Colonel Joseph L. Ryan

1965 None but the Brave - Chief Pharmacist Mate (Directed by Sinatra.)

1966 Assault on a Queen - Mark Brittain

1966 Cast a Giant Shadow - Vince Talmadge

1966 The Oscar - Himself

1967 Tony Rome - Tony Rome

1967 The Naked Runner - Sam Laker

1968 The Detective - Det. Sgt. Joe Leland

1968 Lady In Cement - Tony Rome

1970 Dirty Mingus Magee - Dingus Billy Magee

1980 The First Deadly Sin - Sgt. Edward Delaney

1984 Cannonball Run II - Himself

1988 Who Framed Roger Rabbit? - Singing Sword (vocal)

Documentaries: as himself

1935 Major Bowes Amateur Theatre of the Air

1941 Las Vegas Nights

1942 Ship Ahoy

1943 Reveille with Beverly

1943 Show Business at War

1943 Upbeat in Music (scenes deleted)

1944 Higher and Higher

1944 Road to Victory

1945 A Thousand and One Nights (voice)

1945 The All-Star Bond Rally

1945 MGM Christmas Trailer

1947 Screen Snapshots: Out-of-This-World Series

1948 Lucky Strike Salesman's Movie 48-A

1952 Screen Snapshots: Hollywood Night Life

1954 Three Coins in the Fountain (voice)

1956 Person to Person

1956 Screen Snapshots: Playtime in Hollywood

1959 Invitation to Monte Carlo

1959 Premier Khrushchev in the USA

1962 Sinatra in Israel

1962 Advise and Consent

1964 Paris - When It Sizzles (voice)

1965 A Tribute to the Will Rogers Memorial Hospital

1974 That's Entertainment!

1974 Rene Simard in Japan

1978 The Dean Martin Celebrity Roast: Frank Sinatra

1990 Listen Up: The Lives of Quincy Jones

1993 In Person (voice)

1994 Sinatra: Duets

1995 Sinatra: 80 Years My Way

2006 Sinatra: Vegas

Television cameos

1963 Burke's Law

1970 Make Room for Granddaddy

1987 Magnum, P.I.

1989 Who's the Boss?

1993 Daddy Dearest

Television series

1950/52 The Frank Sinatra Show (CBS)

1957/58 The Frank Sinatra Show (ABC)

1959 The Frank Sinatra Timex Show (ABC)

1959 The Frank Sinatra Timex Show: An Afternoon With Frank Sinatra (ABC)

1960 The Frank Sinatra Timex Show: Here's To The Ladies (ABC)

1960 The Frank Sinatra Timex Show: Welcome Home Elvis (ABC)

Television specials

1965 A Man and His Music

1966 A Man and His Music - Part II

1967 A Man and His Music + Ella + Jobim

1968 Francis Albert Sinatra Does His Thing

1969 Sinatra

1971 Sinatra in Concert at the Royal Festival Hall

1973 Ol' Blue Eyes is Back

1974 The Main Event - Live

1976 John Denver and Friend

1977 Sinatra and Friends

1980 The First Forty Years

1981 The Man and His Music

1982 Concert for the Americas

1985 Portrait of an Album

1985 Sinatra in Japan

Television films

1955 Our Town

1977 Contract on Cherry Street

1995 Young at Heart

Frank Sinatra, Filmography

Written By Michael O'Neill

Michael A. O'Neill is a writer, actor and translator of German books and other texts into English. He studied drama at the Royal Central School in London and for many years wrote, produced and directed historical documentary TV programmes on themes ranging from the ancient Greeks to WWII. These have been broadcast worldwide on a variety of TV channels such as the Discovery Channel and the History Channel. Michael also produced, scripted and composed the music for the TV series 'Hitler's War', and has written novels and newspaper articles. He has written many books on a variety of topics including fashion, music and football, including a biography of Alexander McQueen. Amongst the books he has translated from German are: 'In the Trenches of WWI A German Soldier Remembers', 'Franziska' and 'The War Letters of German and Austrian Jews, 1914'.